John Arnold is a lecturer in Accounting at the University of Manchester. He qualified as a chartered accountant in 1967 (prize-winner in the Intermediate and Final examinations of the Institute of Chartered Accountants in England and Wales). After a short period in practice the author spent two years as Teaching Fellow at the London School of Economics and Political Science, where his interest in decision making problems was stimulated. In 1969 he was awarded an M.Sc. in Accounting and Finance (with distinction) by the University of London. He spent two years at the University of Kent and took up his present appointment in October 1971. His current research interests include the treatment of inflation in management accounting problems, the use of accounting conventions in published accounting statements and methods of pricing.

The purpose of this book is to explain the reasoning behind some of the more useful of the current 'management techniques' and to illustrate their possible practical applications. John Arnold is particularly concerned with the problems of short term decisions. In his discussion he draws heavily upon the methodology of economics and attempts to adapt it to the needs of the modern business man. A significant conclusion of this discussion is the author's recommendation of 'opportunity cost' as the best measure of the economic costs and consequences of decision alternatives. This book will be of interest to both the practical man and the academic.

Modern Finance Series   Editors: *Peter Bird*   Professor of Accounting
                                              University of Kent
                           Bryan Carsberg Professor of Accounting
                                              University of Manchester
                           John Flower   Professor of Accounting
                                              University of Bristol

Pricing and Output Decisions

John Arnold
Lecturer in Accounting
University of Manchester

Accountancy Age Books

312464

Accountancy Age Books
Published by:
Haymarket Publishing Limited
Gillow House
5 Winsley Street
London W1A 2HG
First Published 1973
© Haymarket Publishing Limited
SBN 0 900442 40 9

HD
69
·D4 A75
1973

Printed in Great Britain by
A Wheaton and Company
143 Fore Street
Exeter EX4 3AP
Devon

Contents

8 Dual Prices 123

9 Pricing Problems 135

10 Some Specialised Analytical Models 153

11 Conclusion 171

Index 179

Preface

The Modern Finance Series has been designed with three main purposes in mind. A large proportion of books used in the United Kingdom on advanced courses in accounting are written in the United States. They are deficient because they are set against the background of a legal and institutional environment different from our own. We aim to alleviate this deficiency. Secondly, we aim to present the best current academic thought on important problems in accounting in a form that will be useful to practitioners of accounting and financial management. Thirdly, we aim to contribute to the debate arising out of the recently recognised need to reappraise many accounting procedures.

The best practice in managerial accounting has changed dramatically during the last twenty years. Traditional accounting methods of cost analysis for decision purposes have had to be adapted to new procedures. A primary influence has, perhaps, been that of the operational researcher, who studies business problems by developing mathematical models which describe the relationships between the relevant variables. Furthermore, several of the concepts of the economist have been found helpful in illuminating principles which are relevant for decisions in business. The accountant does not need to became an expert economist or mathematician. He does, however,

need to be able to communicate with experts in these subjects so that
he can co-operate with them in giving advice on business decisions;
he needs to have a basic understanding of the techniques of the
economist or business mathematician so that he can appreciate the
nature of their financial information requirements.

John Arnold's book will help the accountant to meet these
new demands. Without using advanced mathematics, he explains the
nature of business models and illustrates their application to short-term
decisions familiar to the management accountant, in particular the
planning of pricing policy and output levels. In doing so, he reveals
both the strengths and weaknesses of traditional accounting procedures.

Department of Accounting and   BRYAN CARSBERG
    Business Finance
University of Manchester

Introduction

In an increasingly complex business environment there is no shortage
of literature advising firms of the best way to go about achieving their
objectives. The purpose of this book is to explain the reasoning behind
some of the more useful of the current 'management techniques'
and to illustrate how they might be applied in practice. Decision
making is a large and complex area. In a short book it is impossible to
explore its problems fully. For this reason, I have concentrated on a
particular sphere of decision making; the part that is concerned with
short term decisions. This involves considering such problems as: What is
the economic cost of each of the firm's activities? Should it be charging
more or less for its products? What is the best output level for each
product? Is the answer different if resources are in short supply? At
what price should new products be offered? How should overhead
costs be allocated? Indeed should they be allocated? How useful are
traditional accounting data as information to help the decision
maker? These and similar questions are discussed.

It is significant that this discussion should result (as it does in
this book) in the recommendation of 'opportunity cost' as the best
measure of the economic costs and consequences of decision alternatives.
We owe the 'opportunity cost' concept to economists. It is my opinion
that the methodology of economics has much to offer to decision makers.

In this book, I have attempted to draw on that methodology and to adapt it to the needs of the modern business man. The result will, I hope, be of interest and use to both the practical man and the academician.

I have assumed that the reader will have a general (although not detailed) knowledge of accounting and economics. An elementary knowledge of mathematics should also prove helpful, although it is not essential to an understanding of the main principles discussed in the text.

Many friends have helped, directly and indirectly, in the preparation of this book. My interest in the problems of decision making was stimulated initially by colleagues at the London School of Economics during my period there as a Teaching Fellow. Particular thanks are due to Professors Harold Edey and Will Baxter who provided much help during my first years in academic life. I am also grateful to colleagues and students at the University of Manchester for the many stimulating discussions we have enjoyed. In particular, I am indebted to Professor Bryan Carsberg, who provided innumerable valuable comments on an earlier draft and who has been a continual source of encouragement during the writing and revision of the book. Needless to say, responsibility for any errors that remain is mine alone.

Thanks are also due to Maureen Scapens and Colette White who were ingenious enough to turn my original draft into typescript. Last, but by no means least, my thanks go affectionately to my wife Judy, who has spent more than the usual number of solitary evenings during the preparation of this book.

1 A Framework for Decision Making

Decision making is concerned with the basic problem of resource
allocation. This is true whatever the nature of the economic unit
making the decision. For example, we may consider the Government
faced with a decision as to where to site a new airport. It has to
decide how best to utilise available resources needed to construct and
run the airport; for example, land, labour and construction materials.
In such a situation, the Government is unlikely to be constrained by a
limited supply of resources, at least provided it does not require them
over a short interval of time. However, as a competitor with other
potential users of the resources, it may have to pay an increasing price
for increasing amounts of them. In the world as a whole there is a
physical limit on the amount available of any resource and the price
mechanism should serve to allocate the available supply to those
buyers willing to pay the highest prices. The Government's ability to
obtain resources depends on the money it has available to pay for
them; it may be faced with a situation of limited or 'scarce' resources.

　　In principle, the problem facing all economic units is the same;
the optimal allocation of scarce resources. As an example of a very
different kind from that of the Government, we might consider the
case of the small shopkeeper with a limited amount of storage space,
faced with the decision whether to fill it with Brand X or Brand Y

detergent. He, too, must consider the relative merits of the alternative uses of his scarce resource. Given the limited amount which may be stored, will Brand X or Brand Y produce the greater profit?

A further brief examination of these two problems shows that the criteria used in assessing the relative merits of the alternatives may differ between the Government and the small shopkeeper. The latter, in common with most other private sector enterprises, will probably be interested mainly in financial costs and revenues.[1] The Government, however, is often concerned with costs and benefits that cannot readily be measured in financial terms. For example, by providing lighthouses which create financial costs but no direct financial revenues, the Government demonstrates its willingness to undertake projects that yield no financial return but are, presumably, socially desirable. The Government is able to undertake investments that would be rejected in the private sector because of their lack of financial return. It does not need to fear the risk of bankruptcy if financial costs exceed financial revenues, because it has power to raise finance by taxation. Whilst a detailed study of public sector decision making is outside the scope of this text, many of the principles that are relevant for private sector decision making may also be applied in the public sector. The peculiarity of the public sector is the preponderance of costs and benefits for which market values are not appropriate measures.[2] Our primary purpose is to consider decision making in the private sector and this itself involves looking at both financial and 'non-financial' costs and benefits.

1.1   The Need for a Theory of Decision Making
Firms of all sizes and individuals are confronted with three basic financial decisions:

(1)   The *investment* decision. How many of the firm's resources should be committed to investment, that is, sacrificed immediately in return for the expectation of increased resources being available

1. Private sector objectives are discussed at greater length in Chapter 2.
2. For a good introduction to public sector problems see PREST, A R and TURVEY, R, 'Cost-Benefit Analysis: A Survey', in Surveys of Economic Theory, Volume III, Macmillan, 1968.

at some time in the future? Which particular projects should be undertaken with the amounts available for investment?

(2) The *financing* decision. How much finance should the firm raise to enable it to undertake its investment and distribution policies? From what sources should this finance be obtained: retained earnings, issue of ordinary share capital, issue of debentures and so on?

(3) The *distribution* decision. How much of the available resources should be distributed to the proprietor(s) of the business? In the case of the small unlimited business a decision must be made as to how much the proprietors may withdraw from the business. The directors of a limited company face a similar decision in deciding how much of the current funds should be distributed to shareholders as dividend.

These three decisions cannot rationally be taken in isolation of each other. The amount to be committed to investment will depend on the return available on investment opportunities. It will also be a function of the cost and availability of finance and of the distributions required by the proprietors. Similarly, the financing decision will depend on the cost of finance and on available investment opportunities and desired distribution patterns. The distribution decision will depend on investment and financing opportunities.

It is desirable to undertake a continual review of policy in these three areas; if no action is taken the implied decision is to maintain the *status quo*. Our task is to formulate a plan of action that best satisfies the firm's objectives. Do we need to develop a theory to accomplish this task, a theory that draws on the available tools and techniques of scientific method? Many business men apparently attain satisfactory levels of performance by using experience, hunch and intuition. What need have they of a theory? The clue to the answer appears to lie in not regarding the two approaches as mutually exclusive; the question is not whether we should use intuition and experience, or scientific method but whether scientific method is able to complement the inherent skills of the business man in such a way as to lead to better decisions. Later in this chapter, when discussing the use of models in decision making, it will be argued that by applying

scientific method to his problems, the business man will be better
equipped to make decisions consistent with his objectives.

Prior to the 1950's little of an analytical nature had been written
about the problems of decision making in practical business
applications. Most of the available material was essentially descriptive,
concerned with the techniques currently being used by accountants to
record and report on financial performance. Only rarely was
convincing justification provided for the techniques being described.
During the last twenty years a more rigorous body of literature on
decision making has appeared. New techniques, capable of justification
on theoretical grounds, have been developed to fill the need created by
an increasingly complex business environment, characterised by
numerous large scale investments and rapid technological obsolescence.
The rapid growth of computers has enabled the complicated
calculations that are required, to be performed swiftly and accurately.
There is a cost attached to this greater degree of refinement, particularly
where computer time is required. Whether the benefits so derived
outweigh the costs involved is another decision facing the business man.

1.2   The Contribution of the Economist

Any modern author on accounting ignores at his peril the contribution
that has been made by the economist. Many of the problems of central
concern to the accountant have been widely discussed in the economic
literature; for example, income measurement, valuation, cost
calculation, pricing and capital expenditure decisions. Nevertheless, as
a descriptive model of decision making in the firm, standard economic
theory may be criticised. Most economists, with some notable exceptions,[3]
have been concerned primarily with developing theories not to prescribe
decision making procedures for firms but to explain how the price
system functions in allocating resources. Nor have they approached the
latter task by studying in detail the firm's actual decision making
procedures: their theories assume that, in such matters as pricing and
output decisions, market considerations dominate the internal structure

3. See BUCHANAN, J M, Cost and Choice, Markham Publishing Co., 1969,
     Chapter 2, for examples of economists who have attempted to apply
     economic concepts to practical business problems.

of the firm. This has been called the 'black box' philosophy of standard economic theory. Figure 1.1 describes the approach that is implied by this outlook. As a descriptive model of decision making by the firm it may be inappropriate on a number of grounds.

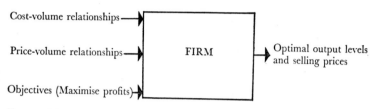

FIGURE 1.1

First, only one objective is normally assumed, namely profit maximisation. This assumption is sometimes inconsistent with empirical observation. In practice, it seems that firms often have a number of goals of which attaining a *satisfactory* level of profit is only one. If we accept the objective of profit maximisation, a further problem arises in defining it. Are we to maximise profit as shown in the conventionally prepared profit and loss account or is some other measure appropriate? This problem is considered further in Chapter 2.

Secondly, basic traditional economic theory rests on an assumption of certainty; that is, the decision maker is aware of the existence and consequences of all present and future investment opportunities. In reality, any individual will be able to observe only a small part of the whole world. Even then his observation of that part may be distorted or he may draw incorrect inferences about the rest of the world from the small part that he is able to see. This is part of the general problem of uncertainty which is inherent in all problems concerned with the future especially in the area of decision making.

Thirdly, traditional economic theory is primarily concerned with determining equilibrium prices and output levels. Our concern is with the path that leads to an equilibrium situation. Traditional theory tells us where we should arrive; it is of less help in telling us how to get there. In a world of continually changing environments the route will be complex.

These criticisms are not meant to condemn economic theory, but to illustrate the difficulties of applying the work of economists to solving problems of decision making in firms. It would be unjust to imply that economists are unaware of the particular difficulties facing the business man. The fact remains, however, that most economists have been primarily concerned with explaining the working of the price system in allocating resources.

Micro-economic theory may not provide a complete solution to the problems of decision making, but the concepts and methodology that economists have developed over the years are of great assistance in constructing a theory of decision making in firms.

1.3   Risk and Uncertainty

In the previous section the problem of risk and uncertainty was introduced. It is convenient to distinguish between the difficulties of estimating and handling the uncertainty inevitably attached to observations of the present and predictions about the future on the one hand and the application of scientific method to the available data after they have been adjusted for uncertainty on the other. It is the second problem, determining the methodology to be used in decision making, that is the main concern of this text. However, no discussion of decision theory is satisfactory without some introductory remarks on the problem of risk and uncertainty.[4]

Traditionally, a distinction is often drawn between risk and uncertainty. A risk situation is defined as one in which there are several possible outcomes and there is material statistical evidence

4. For a more comprehensive introduction to the treatment of and problems inherent in risk and uncertainty see, for example, FRIEDMAN, M and SAVAGE, L J, 'The Utility Analysis of Choices involving Risk', *Journal of Political Economy*, 1948; HIRSHLEIFER, J, 'Investment Decision under Uncertainty: Choice-Theoretic Approaches', *Quarterly Journal of Economics*, November 1965; GRAYSON, C J, Decisions Under Uncertainty: Drilling Decisions by Oil and Gas Operators, Division of Research, Harvard Business School, 1960, Part 2 and Epilogue; GRAYSON, C J, 'The Use of Statistical Techniques in Capital Budgeting', in ROBICHEK, A A (ed), Financial Research and Management Decisions, John Wiley & Sons, 1967; and ROBICHEK, A A and MYERS, S C, Optimal Financing Decisions, Prentice-Hall, 1965, Chapter 5.

relating to them. Risks are normally capable of being insured. Uncertainty is said to exist where there are again several possible outcomes but where there is little previous statistical evidence to guide the decision maker in predicting them. Most business decision problems fall into this category. The distinction between risk and uncertainty in decision making situations seems to be of little practical assistance and henceforth the terms will be used interchangeably.

Among the more refined theories developed for handling uncertainty are a number that make use of the classical concept of probability. These theories avoid some problems encountered in other methods where, for example, figures of most likely outcomes are used to appraise investment opportunities. Theories that use probabilities do not ignore the range of possible outcomes or the likelihood and size of deviations from the most likely results. Probability is strictly defined as the long run relative frequency of a particular event; it may be used to produce a calculation of expected value or expected profit, that is, the long run average profit expected if a particular course of action is undertaken many times. A simple decision rule would involve accepting projects with positive expected profits. Let us consider an example which illustrates this approach.

Suppose that a firm has undertaken a particular business activity 150 times, with the results shown in Table 1.1. It is considering whether it should continue to undertake it. Assume that no changes are expected in the conditions affecting the activity. The probabilities of each outcome, based on previous experience, are as shown in the final column of Table 1.1. The expected value or expected profit of the activity is found by multiplying each outcome by its probability and summing the results:

$$\text{Expected value} = \pounds[-1,000(0.04) - 100(0.12) + 100(0.20) + 150(0.36)$$
$$+ 250(0.18) + 300(0.10)]$$
$$= \pounds97.$$

If the activity is undertaken a sufficient number of times the firm will expect it to produce, on average, a profit of £97 each time. This suggests that it is worthwhile for the firm to continue with the activity.

Table 1.1

Profit/(Loss) £	Number of times Profit/ (Loss) has occurred	Probability of Occurrence
(1,000)	6	$\dfrac{6}{150} = 0.04$
(100)	18	$\dfrac{18}{150} = 0.12$
100	30	$\dfrac{30}{150} = 0.20$
150	54	$\dfrac{54}{150} = 0.36$
250	27	$\dfrac{27}{150} = 0.18$
300	15	$\dfrac{15}{150} = 0.10$
	150	1.00

Suppose, however, that there is only one more chance to undertake the project. Would the firm necessarily want to undertake it again, even though its expected value is positive? The answer will depend on the attitude of the firm's owners to risk and uncertainty. Some firms may be unwilling to run the risk, even though it is small, of incurring a loss of £1,000. Others may be willing to do so as the probability of some profit is high. Different individuals have differing attitudes to uncertainty and it may help to attempt to quantify these attitudes in the decision analysis. Models have been developed that illustrate what is required, but only limited progress has so far been made in applying these models to practical situations.[5]

Unfortunately, most business decision problems are concerned

5. See, for example, FRIEDMAN, M and SAVAGE, L J, 'The Utility Analysis of Choices involving Risk', *Journal of Political Economy*, 1948; and GRAYSON, C J, Decisions under Uncertainty: Drilling Decisions by Oil and Gas Operators, Division of Research, Harvard Business School, 1960, Part 2 and Epilogue.

with opportunities that may be undertaken only once, or a small number of times, and in these cases probability theory is of limited usefulness. Strictly, there is inadequate evidence from which to derive the probabilities. Some advances have been made on the strict application of probability theory which, without providing a completely satisfactory answer, recognise the weaknesses of existing methods of dealing with uncertainty and endeavour to provide solutions which are of some practical assistance.[6]

Perhaps the practically most useful of the means currently available for decisions under uncertainty is sensitivity analysis. This involves calculating the expected pay-off from a project on the basis of most likely outcomes and subsequently investigating the implications of various deviations of actual outcomes from forecast. For example, the value that a particular variable will take if the profit expected from the project is to be reduced to zero may be ascertained and the difference in value expressed as a percentage of its most likely value. This provides an indication of the sensitivity of the project's expected profit to changes in the value of individual variables and points to those estimates in which a small deviation may be critical for the success or failure of the project. These estimates should be examined most carefully before a decision is made on the project. The increased availability of electronic computers and other calculating devices has made this method generally practicable.

1.4   The Use of Models in Decision Making

A model is an approximation or a simulation of real world conditions, constructed from assumed or observed relationships. It may be defined as a set of assumptions from which a conclusion or a set of conclusions is logically deduced. The need for models is twofold. Man is inquisitive by nature and if he observes phenomena that he is unable to explain intuitively, he feels a need for further investigation of the causes of the phenomena.

6. Two articles in this category are HERTZ, D B. 'Risk Analysis in Capital Investment', *Harvard Business Review*, Vol. 42, No. 1, January–February, 1964 and HILLIER, F S, 'The Derivation of Probabilistic Information for the Evaluation of Risky Investments', *Management Science*, Vol. 9, No. 3, April, 1963.

This desire to explain is one *raison d'etre* of models. The second purpose, not unrelated to the first, is a need to predict; decisions have to be made and if they are to be rational we want to know what consequences will flow from each available course of action. It is a moot point whether it is necessary for decision purposes that a model should explain as well as predict. Our confidence in a particular model may be enhanced if we are able to understand why it appears to be a good predictor. But there is no obvious reason to reject a model that predicts well, merely because we are unable to understand why it does so.

The methodology of constructing and testing models is essentially the same for both the natural and the social sciences. We may distinguish between physical and abstract models. Physical models are material representations of some real world state which is to be analysed either for the purpose of explanation or to predict reactions in the real world situation itself. An example of such a model is to be found at the recently established training school for oil tanker captains. Scale models of oil tankers, displaying characteristics similar to those of real tankers, are available to potential tanker captains for navigation through scaled down waterways to prepare them for the real world problems involved in handling large vessels.

Most economic models are not physical models. There are obvious difficulties in constructing physical replicas of economic situations. Instead, more abstract models are used. These may take the form of verbal expressions, geometric diagrams or, most frequently, mathematical expressions. All of these forms of abstract models may be expressed in computer language. Let us consider an example of an abstract model taking the form of a mathematical expression. A company wishes to predict its profit for the coming year. It manufactures only one product which it sells at a fixed unit price. There are two types of cost associated with the manufacture and sale of the product: those that vary directly with the level of production and sale and those that are fixed regardless of the quantity manufactured or sold.[7] The

7. We shall assume for simplicity that stock levels are to remain constant during the year and consequently the quantity produced will equal the quantity sold.

following mathematical expression predicts the firm's profit for the coming year:

$$X = Py - (F + Vy)$$

where X = the profit we wish to predict
P = the (constant) selling price per unit
F = the total fixed costs for the coming year
V = the variable cost per unit produced and sold
y = the predicted quantity to be manufactured and sold.

To calculate X we need to estimate values for P, F, V and y. Suppose these estimated values are $P = £15$, $F = £4,500$, $V = £7.5$ and $y = 1,000$ units. We may predict the profit for the coming year by substituting these values in our original expression:

$$X = £15(1,000) - (£4,500 + £7.5[1,000])$$
$$= £3,000.$$

In the original expression Py represents the total revenue in the coming year and $(F + Vy)$ the total costs. We could, without altering the predicted value of X, rearrange the terms to emphasise the difference between fixed and variable costs:

$$X = (P - V)y - F.$$

In this expression $(P - V)y$ represents what is often referred to as the gross margin and what we shall call, in later chapters, the total contribution to fixed costs and profit. F, as before, represents the total predicted fixed costs for the year.

The cost and revenue behaviour implied by this model is unlikely to apply in such a simple form to many real world situations. In practice there is invariably a conflict in using the model building approach. On the one hand, enough information should be included to avoid the model being so unrepresentative of the real world situation that its predictions have little more than random accuracy. On the other, sufficient simplification must be introduced to enable the consequences of various courses of action to be isolated and analysed using the available computational facilities. This simplification of the real world, which is inherent in all models, is both their greatest strength and weakness.

1.5   A General Decision Model

The previous section introduced in general terms the application of the scientific method of model building to decision making. Let us now turn to a more detailed consideration of the likely stages that would be involved in constructing a decision making model for a particular firm. Figure 1.2 provides an outline of the various steps. There are likely to be inter-relationships between some of the stages other than those outlined. For the sake of simplicity only those relationships that are considered fundamental have been included.

The first stage in the decision process will normally be to establish the firm's objectives. Without knowing where we are aiming for, it is difficult to plan strategies to take us there.

The second stage will probably involve a review of current operating performance and a comparison with the desired state. If current performance appears to correspond with the firm's objectives, one of two things might happen. First, the mere fact of attainment may cause the firm to increase its aspiration level; the achievement of some desired level of performance may cause it to strive for something better. Objectives will be altered and the search will commence for investment opportunities to bridge the gap between the current position and the revised goals. Alternatively the firm may be satisfied with its current performance and decide to leave things as they are.[8]

If the current situation fails to comply with the stated objectives then the firm will proceed to the third stage in the process outlined in Figure 1.2. It will search for decision alternatives, for example, productive or investment opportunities, with the property of narrowing the gap between current and desired performance. It will also seek information about the possible future environments in which it will be

8. If the assumed objective is profit maximisation it is unlikely that the firm will ever be able to establish whether it is meeting this goal. It will be constrained by inadequate and imperfect information from assessing whether it could improve its current situation in terms of a profit maximising objective. An objective of, say, a profit of £2,000 per annum and a working week of less than 35 hours could more readily be checked against current performance.

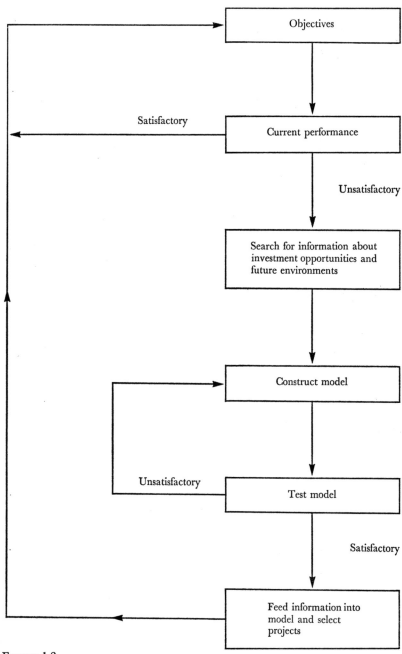

FIGURE 1.2

operating. There will be more than one possible environment, i.e. there will be uncertainty.

Having defined objectives, reviewed the current situation and gathered information about decision alternatives and likely future environments, the firm may proceed to construct a model. This model will predict the effects of the various decision alternatives on the measures represented in the stated objectives in the various environments that might obtain. For example, the model might predict the effect of accepting a particular investment opportunity.

Before the model is used to select the combination of opportunities that seems to satisfy best the firm's objectives it should be checked critically to discover whether it is appropriate for that particular firm and predicts efficiently when applied to the firm's affairs. In the natural sciences, it is often possible to conduct controlled laboratory experiments to test a model. This is more difficult in the social sciences; the subjects of the experiments are human beings whose reactions may be affected by the very fact that they have been chosen as subjects of the experiment.[9] Consequently, to test a decision model it may be necessary to make use of historical data, trying to ensure that the historical circumstances are similar to those expected in the future. If the model performs satisfactorily under test conditions, we may move to the final stage in the decision process. If not, we must review the construction stage in an attempt to impart the requisite validity.

The final stage in the process involves feeding current information about decision alternatives and future environments into the model and selecting that combination of opportunities which the model reveals to be in best accord with the firm's objectives. The process does not end there. It continues so long as the firm exists. New decision alternatives become apparent and more information emerges about the future environments facing the firm. These must be fed into the model so that a new optimal plan may be calculated. The firm's objectives may change, particularly in the light of performance achieved. The process of adapting the model and of revising the

9. For examples of these difficulties see LUPTON, TOM, Management and the Social Sciences, Penguin, 1971, Chapters 1 and 2.

optimal plan is continuous; the decision making environment is dynamic and any decision making model that is to be of value must be able to reflect this.

What has been said above relates to a general decision model that broadly covers the decision making process of the firm. In practice the firm may also have a number of other decision models relating, for example, to particular aspects of its business. The situation is almost exactly similar to the budgeting procedure of the firm where numerous departmental, divisional and sectional budgets are combined to form the master budget of the whole firm. There are strong interdependences between the individual budgets just as there will be between the various models operative within the firm.

For example, a firm may have models predicting stockholding costs, relationships between sellings prices and quantities demanded, the behaviour of production costs as production quantities change, and so on. The models are interdependent; to determine an optimal production plan the predicted relationships between stockholding and production costs and sales revenue as production volumes change must be considered together. It is useful to illustrate this point further in terms of the uses of maps, another particular example of models. There may be many different maps of a particular area, concentrating on different special features, such as climate, population, industry and so on, each one useful for a particular purpose.

In the same way there may be various decision models used in a firm, each one being constructed according to the purpose for which it is required, with varying emphases and differing degrees of detail. We have outlined the procedure to be followed if models are to be used in decision making. Before moving on to consider this sort of decision methodology in more detail, we shall attempt to justify its use, as an aid to managerial experience. There appear to be four major advantages from using models as aids to decision making.

First is the increase in speed with which decisions may be taken; the framework has been established and for many routine decisions all that is required is to 'plug in' the relevant figures to the existing model, which will then produce the information on the basis of which the decision may be quickly taken.

Secondly, because the basic model is established, the decisions to which it leads should be consistent, even in complex situations. Given the selection criteria, the probability of an inferior (that is inferior in terms of the firm's objectives) opportunity being accepted in preference to a superior one should be lower than if no methodological approach is used.

The qualities of rationality and consistency lead to the third advantage, the ability to delegate. When the decision process is explicit, subordinates are better equipped to make decisions demonstrably consistent with the objectives of the firm and, presumably, with the wishes of top management. This is an advantage that assumes greater importance as a business grows and the chief executive or proprietor finds it increasingly difficult to make all decisions himself.

The final advantage is possibly the most important. In constructing and using models the decision maker is forced to consider explicitly relationships that have previously been implicit. Model building, after all, is no more than the formalisation of processes that are used intuitively by good business men. But the sheer volume of data needed to make decisions is enough to defeat most of us if we have to choose between alternative courses of action with no explicit guidelines to help us. The formalisation of the assumptions, values and inter-relationships that the decision maker carries around in his head, may itself reveal hitherto unsuspected information that will improve the quality of decision making.

There are also disadvantages associated with the model building approach. The cost factor has already been mentioned; if the decision making process itself is complicated then the calculations necessary to determine an optimal plan will also be complex and may require the use of an electronic digital computer or some other mechanical device.

Secondly, there is the danger inherent in all mathematical solutions that they suggest an illusory precision. The output from a model is unlikely to be more accurate than the input data used. This should be borne in mind when the output is being analysed.

Finally, we should again mention that some benefits and costs are not easily accommodated in the essentially quantitative approach outlined above. For example, the proprietor of a small business may regard one free afternoon a week to play golf as highly desirable but may have considerable difficulty in quantifying the benefit he receives. In such areas value judgements by decision makers are essential complements to the use of models.

We have noted that the use of models has powerful advantages, and some disadvantages which may be reduced by appropriate precautions in use. We cannot say that the cost of complex models is always worthwhile, but we shall proceed on the assumption that it will often be so and that the model building approach is at least worth investigation.

2 The Development of a Decision Model

2.1   A Business Decision Model

The importance of establishing objectives prior to embarking on the decision making process was discussed in Chapter 1. The objective of each individual, and hence of the proprietors of a firm, will be to maximise satisfaction (which we shall call consumption) over time.[1] Broadly speaking, the goods and services of which consumption consists are only available in return for the payment of a cash price. Consequently we shall build a decision model using an assumed objective of 'maximising' future consumption potential (normally cash): the decision rule will be to accept opportunities that increase the value of future cash resources and to reject those that decrease it.[2] In a subsequent section we shall consider alternatives to the objective assumed here.

1. At this stage we shall assume that the firms under consideration exclude limited liability companies (whose dividend policies may create particular problems).
2. Certain benefits and costs that accrue to the proprietors of a firm cannot be expressed readily in cash terms, for example status, personal job satisfaction and freedom of choice regarding hours of work. To simplify the exposition the analysis will be undertaken at this stage solely in terms of cash flows. Where non-cash benefits and costs arise in future examples suggestions will be made for handling them.

19

We shall make two simplifying assumptions before constructing the model. First, we shall assume that there are perfect markets for borrowing and lending funds; that is, perfect capital markets. Three conditions must be met if this assumption is to hold:

(i)   No lender or borrower is large enough for his transactions to affect the ruling market price for funds (the interest rate).

(ii)   All traders in the market have equal and costless access to information about the ruling price and all other relevant information.

(iii)   There are no transaction costs involved in using the market and no taxes that would alter economic decisions.

Secondly, we shall assume that there is certainty about the future (see Chapter 1, pages 6–9). If these two assumptions hold, there will be an unique market rate of interest, which we shall call i, at which all users of the capital market are able to borrow or lend as much as they wish.[3] This condition leads to a useful simplification in the analysis; it enables us to compare cash flows which arise at different points in time by using a general unique rate of interest. The need to use an interest rate arises because individuals would not normally be indifferent between £X receivable immediately and the certainty of £X to be received at some time in the future. Discrimination may be caused by the existence of investment opportunities, the cost of borrowing funds or a preference for immediate rather than future consumption.

Given the unique market rate of interest, i, an individual presently in possession of £C could lend it to yield £$C\,(1+i)$ after one year. Alternatively, an individual wanting to invest an amount now to yield £C in a year's time need invest only £$C/(1+i)$. A rational individual, because of the lending and borrowing opportunities available to him, would be indifferent between the certainty of £C to be received in one year's time and £$C/(1+i)$ receivable immediately. By using no more than compound interest methods, we are able to compare amounts of cash arising at different points in time.

3. Under the conditions assumed, competitive forces are likely to eliminate opportunities to lend or borrow at any interest rate other than i.

The value now (or *present value*) to the above individual of £C receivable in one year is £$C/(1 + i)$.

Suppose an individual or firm is entitled to a stream of cash flows: $C_1, C_2, C_3, \ldots, C_n, \ldots$, representing the net cash receivable at the end of year 1, 2, 3, $\ldots, n, \ldots$, respectively. The present value, V_0, of this stream of cash flows to the individual or firm may be described by the expression:

$$V_0 = \frac{C_1}{(1 + i)} + \frac{C_2}{(1 + i)^2} + \frac{C_3}{(1 + i)^3} + \cdots + \frac{C_n}{(1 + i)^n} + \cdots$$

The above expression may more conveniently be written:[4]

$$V_0 = \sum_{j=1}^{\infty} \frac{C_j}{(1 + i)^j} \tag{1}$$

where C_j is the net cash receivable at the end of year j. If the expression is applied to a particular firm and $\sum_{j=1}^{\infty} C_j$ represents the sum of all of the net cash flows that are expected to accrue to the firm in the future, then V_0, the present value of those cash flows, represents the current value of the firm, based on future consumption potential. What is required is a decision rule to be applied in appraising opportunities or sets of opportunities that will lead us to accept those opportunities that increase V_0 and reject those that decrease V_0.

Suppose that a firm, with a current value V_0 as described in expression (1), is considering whether to accept an investment opportunity requiring an immediate cash outlay of I_0 and producing the following net cash inflows:

$$F_1, F_2, F_3, \ldots, F_n, \ldots$$

4. The Greek letter Σ (sigma) is convenient mathematical shorthand, meaning the sum of all values in a particular series. By introducing lower and upper limits (written below and above Σ) we may define the summation of a particular series between certain limits. So:

$$\sum_{i=1}^{i=n} x_i \left(\text{or} \sum_{i=1}^{n} x_i \right) = x_1 + x_2 + x_3 + \cdots + x_n.$$

where F_1 is the net cash inflow at the end of year 1 and so on. Should the firm accept or reject the opportunity? If V_0' is the value of the firm after it decides to undertake the investment (but before it pays the investment outlay required, I_0) then the firm should **accept the project only if $V_0' > V_0$**, that is if $V_0' - V_0$ is positive. If we add the cash flows arising from the new project to those already expected by the firm we can calculate the revised value of the firm:

$$V_0' = - I_0 + \frac{C_1 + F_1}{(1 + i)} + \frac{C_2 + F_2}{(1 + i)^2} + \cdot \cdot \cdot \cdot + \frac{C_n + F_n}{(1 + i)^n} + \cdot \cdot \cdot \cdot$$

which may be re-written as:

$$V_0' = - I_0 + \sum_{j=1}^{\infty} \frac{C_j + F_j}{(1 + i)^j}$$

or

$$V_0' = - I_0 + \sum_{j=1}^{\infty} \frac{C_j}{(1 + i)^j} + \sum_{j=1}^{\infty} \frac{F_j}{(1 + i)^j} \tag{2}$$

If acceptance of the project is worthwhile, V_0' [expression (2)] $- V_0$ [expression (1)] must be greater than zero:

$$V_0' - V_0 = - I_0 + \sum_{j=1}^{\infty} \frac{C_j}{(1 + i)^j} + \sum_{j=1}^{\infty} \frac{F_j}{(1 + i)^j} - \sum_{j=1}^{\infty} \frac{C_j}{(1 + i)^j}$$

$$V_0' - V_0 = - I_0 + \sum_{j=1}^{\infty} \frac{F_j}{(1 + i)^j}$$

The value of $V_0' - V_0$ will be positive, and the condition $V_0' > V_0$ satisfied, only if:

$$\sum_{j=1}^{\infty} \frac{F_j}{(1 + i)^j} > I_0$$

or

$$\sum_{j=1}^{\infty} \frac{F_j}{(1 + i)^j} - I_0 > 0. \tag{3}$$

The left hand side of inequality (3) is normally called the *net present value* of the project. If this net present value is positive then acceptance of the project should lead to an increase in the consumption potential of the owners of the firm and hence to an increase in the firm's value. If it is negative, acceptance will lead to a decrease in consumption potential and value. Our decision rule for appraising new investment opportunities is to accept those with positive net present values and reject those with negative net present values. The firm will be indifferent between acceptance and rejection of a project with a zero net present value.[5]

   In developing the net present value decision rule we have assumed the existence of perfect capital markets. This is not normally justified in real world conditions, where interest rates may be observed to vary between different groups of lenders and borrowers. If we make more realistic assumptions about the behaviour of capital markets, the general method of analysis outlined above remains applicable. Deciding on the discount rate to be used is the particular problem that becomes more difficult.

2.2   The Business Decision Model and 'Profit Maximisation'

It is apparent from the previous section that there is a close link between maximising satisfaction from consumption and maximising current value. If the current value of an asset, a group of assets, or a firm depends on the future consumption they will allow their owners to enjoy, then the maximisation of future satisfaction is equivalent to the maximisation of current value. Is it equivalent also to the objective of 'profit maximisation', often propounded in both the economic and accounting literature? The answer to this question depends on the definition ascribed to profit.

   Economists and accountants are broadly in agreement as regards one aspect of profit calculation; that there is a link between the profit of a firm and the value of that firm at various points in time.

---

5. For a more detailed theoretical analysis of the net present value decision rule see HIRSHLEIFER, J, 'On the Theory of Optimal Investment Decision', *Journal of Political Economy*, Vol. 66, 1958.

The relationship may be expressed in a simple mathematical form:

$$P_1 = V_1 - V_0 \tag{4}$$

where

P_1 is the profit for period 1
V_1 is the value of the firm at the end of period 1 and
V_0 is the value of the firm at the end of period 0 (the beginning of period 1).

In this simple form it is assumed that no distributions are made to the proprietors and that no capital is introduced by them during period 1. The definition is easily extended to accommodate these possibilities.

If we define D_1 as the distributions made to the proprietors during period 1 and C_1 as the capital introduced by them during the same period, expression (4) may be re-written as follows:

$$P_1 = V_1 - V_0 + D_1 - C_1. \tag{5}$$

Other things being equal, any increase in D_1 will be exactly compensated by a decrease in V_1 and any increase in C_1 will result in a corresponding increase in V_1. Assuming that we are at time 0 (the beginning of period 1) and that therefore V_0 is given, and noting what was said above about changes in D_1 and C_1 being exactly compensated by changes in V_1, the only means available for increasing P_1 is to increase V_1 without having recourse to D_1 or C_1.

What has just been said relates to the measurement of profit during a given period. We can apply the same reasoning to estimating the profitability of a single investment opportunity. If V_0 is the value of a firm before accepting a particular project and V_0' its value after accepting the project, then P', the 'profit' from the project, may be written [adapting expression (4)]:

$$P' = V_0' - V_0. \tag{6}$$

If P' is positive, the project is profitable and should be accepted if the firm's objective is to maximise profits. If V_0' and V_0 are defined as in the previous section [expressions (2) and (1)], being based on cash flow expectations, then P' in expression (6) is equivalent to the net present value of the project [the left hand side of inequality (3)] described in the previous section. In this case, profit maximisation is identical to maximising net present value.

The double-entry approach traditionally employed by accountants accords with the general definition of profit implied by expressions (4), (5) and (6); the profit in the profit and loss account represents the change in the balance sheet value of the organisation, suitably adjusted for distributions and capital introduced. Later in this chapter we shall consider some of the traditional accounting conventions for calculating balance sheet values to see whether they imply useful definitions of profit for decision purposes. First we shall consider briefly some objectives that have been suggested as alternatives to profit maximisation.

2.3   Objectives in the Private Sector

The assumed objective of traditional economic theory is profit maximisation. This need not, and for reasons to be discussed in the next section should not, be equated with the maximisation of the profit disclosed by conventionally prepared accounting statements. However, problems of definition aside, even the concept of maximising the profit of the owners as the sole objective of the firm has been criticised widely in recent years. The grounds for this criticism are broadly empirical. It is argued that the firm is a coalition of groups, each pursuing its own objectives, and each of which is in a position to exert influence on those responsible for taking decisions within the firm. Amongst these groups might be included the proprietors (equity shareholders in the case of a limited company), managers, trade unions, creditors, loan stock and preference shareholders, other employees and government. Traditional economic theory, which implies that all profits accrue to the proprietors with all other members of the firm participating in return for their prevailing market prices, tends to ignore the pressure that groups other than the proprietors are able to exert on the decision maker.

It is further argued on empirical grounds that even proprietors may be interested in goals other than profit goals.[6] It has been suggested, for example, that some firms seek to maximise total sales

6. See, for example, CYERT, R M and MARCH, J G, A Behavioral Theory of the Firm, Prentice-Hall, 1963, page 9.

revenue subject to some minimum profit constraint and that others
have as their primary objective long-run survival or maximisation of
market share. A number of writers have argued that although firms
may be interested in profit their objective is not to maximise it but to
maintain it at a satisfactory level. 'Satisfactory profits represent a level
of aspiration that the firm uses to evaluate alternative policies. The
aspiration level may change over time, but in the short run it defines
a utility function (*measure of satisfaction*) with essentially only two
values—good enough and not good enough.'[7]

The type of firm upon which traditional economic theory is
based is assumed to have no market power and to be equipped with
perfect knowledge. In these circumstances it may be reasonable to
assume an objective of profit maximisation: because of the forces of
competition a firm that fails to maximise profits may eventually be
unable to continue in business. But that sort of firm bears little
resemblance to the large, oligopolistic organisations of modern
industry. Does this mean that we must reject profit maximisation as the
primary objective for our decision model? It has been argued that to
do so, and to include instead some or all of the alternative objectives,
will make creation of new theories virtually impossible with the
mathematical tools presently available.[8] Of itself this argument
provides insufficient reason for accepting what may be an outmoded
goal. However, there may be other justifications for accepting profit
maximisation as a working objective. If we accept the 'coalition of
groups' concept of the firm we might argue that profit maximisation is
the best objective to pursue in order to satisfy all the interested groups.
The difficulty is primarily one of distribution; profit maximisation
should lead to the largest possible cake being available to the firm as a
whole—pressure will not be applied until a decision has to be taken as
to how the cake should be divided.[9]

7. CYERT, R M and MARCH, J G, A Behavioral Theory of the Firm, Prentice-
   Hall, 1963, pages 9–10.
8. PAPANDREOU, A and WHEELER, J, Competition and Its Regulation,
   Prentice-Hall, 1954, pages 73–74.
9. This approach produces its own problems. Some groups in the coalition
   may disagree with others as to how big the cake is, and as to whether it is
   the largest attainable.

One of the leading paladins of traditional economic theory and consequently of profit maximisation is Milton Friedman. He argues that the only true test of a theory is one that is based on its predictive ability, and claims that traditional theory allows good economic predictions to be made about market behaviour.[10] (Apparently, Friedman's claim relates to economy- or industry-wide predictions, not to the behaviour of individual firms.) However, the difficulties involved in empirical testing have caused Friedman's claims to be treated with some caution.

Certain of the other objectives propounded earlier may not be inconsistent with a goal of profit maximisation. For example, the maximisation of market share may not be an end in itself but rather a means of achieving an end of profit maximisation. Similarly the managing director who recommends that company finances be used to buy a Rolls-Royce motor car for his personal transport may not be acting from purely selfish motives. He might reason that the status attached to such a vehicle will so impress potential customers as to raise profits by more than the cost of the Rolls-Royce. Nevertheless, it remains probable that many firms do have goals other than profit maximisation. In this case it might be possible to incorporate these goals in a model that assumes as its dominant objective profit maximisation, by including them as constraints that must not be violated in seeking to achieve the main goal. However, if it is clear that a firm has primary goals other than profit maximisation, then the framework developed previously may be inappropriate. It may be necessary to construct a separate decision model based on the dominant objectives. For the remainder of this text we shall assume that the firm's main goal is to maximise the present value of its expected future net benefits, defined in cash terms where possible.

2.4   The Conventional Accounting Approach

The conventional accounting approach to recording and reporting financial information is important as it is often the main source of data available to those responsible for making decisions. We shall look now

10. FRIEDMAN, M, 'The Methodology of Positive Economics', in Essays in Positive Economics, University of Chicago Press, 1953.

in more detail at some of the conventions used by accountants to see how closely they accord with the valuation model and decision rule discussed previously.

These conventions have emerged from, and been influenced by, a complex of requirements. The most important of these are the calculation of taxation liability, the determination of the amounts available for distribution, and control over the stewardship duties of those responsible for running the firm, including the protection of creditors.[11] These requirements have been responsible for the growth of legal and other doctrines that now have a strong influence on the form and content of traditional accounts: the published profit and loss account and balance sheet. Examples are the Companies Acts, various legal decisions on the amounts available for dividend payments and taxation assessments and recommendations from the professional accountancy bodies. For these purposes conventionally prepared accounts may be adequate. We have to consider their usefulness as part of the general decision process of the firm and, in particular, how well they reflect the principles implied by the valuation model and decision rule developed previously. There are several obvious points of conflict:[12]

(i)   Fixed assets are generally valued at cost less a provision for amortisation of such cost (usually called depreciation). Normally no account is taken of value either in the market or to the proprietors.

(ii)   Certain current assets, for example stock, are valued at the lower of cost and market value. The effect of this is to give recognition to 'unrealised' losses but to ignore 'unrealised' profits.

(iii) 'Intangible' assets, for example goodwill, are often included in the balance sheet only if they have been purchased and even

---

11. For this purpose, stewardship is normally defined in a somewhat limited sense to exclude questions of efficiency.

12. For a more comprehensive critique of accounting conventions see EDWARDS, R S, 'The Nature and Measurement of Income', in BAXTER, W T, and DAVIDSON, S (eds), Studies in Accounting Theory, Sweet and Maxwell, 1962.

then are sometimes written down to a minimal figure. No account is usually taken of the value of these assets.

(iv) A distinction is normally made between capital and revenue items. The latter are included as income while the former are treated as capital profits or losses and excluded from the profit and loss account. This distinction creates the paradoxical situation that recurrent capital profits, for example from the sale of fixed assets, may be excluded from the profit and loss account while non-recurring items, for example the income of a non-repetitive boom year, are included.

(v) The balance sheet value of a firm is the arithmetical total of its assets less its liabilities. However, when two assets, individually valued at say $£X$ and $£Y$, are combined they may be capable of generating cash flows with a higher present value than $£(X + Y)$. This phenomenon, known in the literature on corporate strategy as synergy, is generally ignored in conventionally prepared accounts.

To summarise, the weaknesses of accounting conventions when applied to the solution of decision problems stem from the failure of conventional methods to take account of future expectations in a satisfactory way when determining value. In later examples we shall consider specific cases of conventional data failing to satisfy the needs of our decision rule.

2.5 Restrictions on the Scope of the Study

A number of principles have been mentioned that are central to the decision methodology to be applied to firms in the private sector. To consider all of them in detail in one short book would be impossible. Our main purpose here is to consider the methodology of relatively short term decisions and its practical application. Consequently problems arising specifically from the long term nature of certain investment decisions will be mentioned only briefly: the problem of the optimal allocation of resources *over time* is the problem of capital budgeting which has a separate literature of its own.[13] This is not to

13. See, for example, CARSBERG, B V, Analysis for Investment Decisions, Haymarket Publishing, forthcoming, and FREEAR, J, Financing Decisions in Business, Haymarket Publishing.

say that the methodologies of short term and long term decisions are divorced and should be treated in isolation. Many common principles exist and an attempt to solve short term and long term decision problems separately will probably result in an allocation of resources that is not the best available given the firm's objectives.

In terms of the decision rule developed earlier in this chapter [expression (3)] our problem is to identify and evaluate the benefits and costs $\left(\sum_{j=1}^{\infty} F_j \text{ and } I_0 \right)$ flowing from the various courses of action available to the firm. We are not concerned primarily with decisions that bring costs and benefits spread over a long period of time. We shall not consider the problems of determining a discount rate (the cost of capital) nor shall we discuss the problem of dividend policy in so far as it may affect the value of an organisation. In short, we are concerned with decisions that have only relatively short term consequences of, say, one year or less. The methods suggested are capable of adaptation to the solution of longer term problems.

3 Principles of Cost Evaluation

3.1 Basic Principles of Cost Evaluation

Decisions are concerned with choices between alternatives. If there are no alternatives then there can be no choice and consequently no decision; there is only one path open.[1] Decisions fall into two basic categories: accept or reject decisions and ranking decisions. The former arise when the firm is considering a particular opportunity, the acceptance of which will not preclude acceptance of any other current or potential opportunities that are or might become available.

Ranking decisions are necessary when the firm has to choose between two or more opportunities and is constrained from accepting all of them. This situation will arise either when the firm has insufficient supplies of one or more of its resources to accept all the available opportunities, or when two or more of the investment opportunities are mutually exclusive, that is acceptance of one of them precludes acceptance of the others. As an example of mutually exclusive alternatives we might consider the case of a firm wishing to construct a new factory but being unsure as to whether it should be small, medium or large. Once it decides to choose one of the

1. For this purpose one alternative will normally be to reject the particular project under consideration.

alternatives, say the large factory, the interest in building either a small or medium one probably disappears. The acceptance of one alternative has precluded the acceptance of two others.

The central part of the appraisal is to identify and evaluate the relevant costs and benefits resulting from the various alternatives available to the firm. Much of the discussion will be concerned with the ascertainment of the costs of particular opportunities. This should not be taken to imply that benefits are less important, but merely that systematic analysis normally has to play a smaller role in their estimation. The basic principles to be applied, however, are similar for benefits and costs.

The basic principles of relevant cost are not difficult to derive; they follow from the valuation model and decision rule developed in Chapter 2. However, there is a world of difference between the statement and the application of principles. For this reason extensive use will be made of examples. Cost ascertainment is analogous in this respect to double entry book-keeping: once the principles are mastered their application to diverse situations should present few problems.

Whether or not a particular cost is relevant to a decision will depend on the objectives of the firm, as will the weight to be given to the particular cost. The objective assumed here is the maximisation of the present value of future cash flows accruing to the firm, including any indirect benefits. Consequently, we shall be concerned primarily with the cash costs and benefits expected to result from the various courses of action being considered. This concept of relevant cost may play a smaller part in public sector decisions. The private firm considering how best to transmit electricity will probably choose the method with the lowest cash cost; say, overhead wiring as opposed to underground cables if it is allowed by law to do so. The government, however, faced with the same decision may choose the more expensive (in cash terms) underground cables in order to avoid the social cost associated with the unfortunate scenic effect of pylons and overhead wiring. In the private sector, given the assumptions made previously, the first principle of cost calculation is that we are concerned primarily with the cash consequences of decision alternatives.

The second principle is an extension of the first. Any decision can affect the course only of future events, be they 5 seconds or 5 years away. Nothing we do now can affect anything that has already happened. The costs that are relevant for a decision are future costs; any costs already incurred cannot be affected by any decision that we might make now, and to include them as relevant costs may lead to an incorrect decision. For example, suppose a firm has some stock of raw material that cost £100 two years ago but is now obsolete and unusable in any of the firm's production processes. If the firm is offered £10 for the stock of materials should it accept? To include the original cost of £100 as a relevant cost of the decision would imply a loss of £90 on the transaction and rejection by the firm. Yet other things being equal, and no other purchaser being available, the firm will be £10 better off if it sells the stock than if it does not. The original cost is not relevant to this decision and should not be included as a cost of it. Although past, or historical, costs are not of themselves relevant to decisions within the framework we are using, they may be useful aids to predicting future costs. This application of historical costs is discussed further in Chapter 5.

Although futurity is a necessary condition of relevance in cost calculation it is not a sufficient one. Decisions are concerned with choices between alternatives and a cost that is expected to remain at the same level whichever alternative is chosen should not influence the choice between the alternatives. This is the third basic principle, that only those costs that will differ under some or all of the alternatives need be considered. For example, a commuter may be considering whether to travel to his office by train on five or six occasions during the coming week. Whether he travels five or six times it is cheaper for him to purchase a weekly season ticket than to pay his fares daily. The cost of the season ticket is the same whether he travels five or six times and is not relevant to his choice between the two alternatives. It follows that any apportionment of the cost of the season ticket (say on an 'average cost per journey' basis) is also irrelevant for the decision. The cost would be relevant, however, if a third alternative were to be considered; the possibility of not travelling to the office at all in the coming week. In this situation there would be no need to purchase the season ticket, the cost of which should then be considered as a differential cost relevant to the decision.

From the objective of maximising the present value of future cash flows we have developed three basic principles of cost calculation. First, that we are interested primarily in cash costs; second, that only future costs should be considered and third, that only differential, or incremental, costs are relevant. We should consider only expected future cash flows that will differ under the alternatives available. Before proceeding to an illustration of these principles it should be noted that *all* changes to a firm's cash flow resulting from a particular decision should be taken into account and not just those easily identified with a particular project. If a decision taken in department A of a firm results in department B incurring extra cash costs these must be treated as costs of the decision taken in department A.

Example

Mr Frost owns and occupies a two-storey house in which gas fired central heating is installed to the ground floor only. The first floor is heated by oil convector fires. The original cost of the gas fired central heating was £250 and of the oil heaters, £50. The oil heaters have no resale value. Mr Frost is considering whether to dispose of the oil heaters and extend the gas central heating to cover the whole house. He intends to sell the house in about 3 years and feels that the extension to the central heating will add some £150 to the resale value of the house. He has received a quotation of £200 from a local builder for the extension. The expected annual fuel costs of the part central heating system are £80 as opposed to the annual costs of a full system which are estimated at £150. Fuel and maintenance for the oil heaters costs £50 each year. Mr Frost pays his local Gas Board £15 per annum to service and maintain the part central heating system and does not expect this cost to alter if the system is extended. On the basis of the information given, and ignoring any effect of the timing of the cash flows, we are required to advise Mr Frost whether to proceed with the extension.

An incremental cash flow approach gives the figures in Table 3.1). The difference column provides a convenient means of expressing the cost or incremental cash flow resulting from a particular course of action, in this case the extension of the system. A final form of presentation might have excluded columns (1) and (2) as all of the relevant cash flow information is included in the difference column.

Table 3.1

	(1) Extend system	(2) Retain present system	(1)–(2) Difference
	£	£	£
Cost of extension	−200	0	−200
Extra sales proceeds	+150	0	+150
Fuel costs of gas central heating (3 years)	−450	−240	−210
Running costs of oil heaters (3 years)	0	−150	+150
Central heating service contract (3 years)	− 45	− 45	0
	−545	−435	−110

(Note: a negative symbol indicates a negative cash flow, that is a cash outflow, while a positive symbol represents a positive cash flow or a cash inflow. So in the case of the cost of extension the cash flow involved is −£200, i.e. a cost of £200.)

A more conventional form of presentation of this column might run:

Table 3.2

	£	£
Cost of extension		200
Increase in cost of fuel		210
		410
Less Extra sales proceeds expected as a result of extension	150	
Saving in running costs of oil heaters	150	300
Incremental cost of extending system:		110

Whether we consider this incremental cost statement or the differential cash flow statement from which it is derived, the answer is the same. Over the next 3 years Mr Frost will incur extra costs of £110 if he goes ahead with the proposed extension to his central heating system. Strictly on financial grounds, he should not undertake the extension. The analysis in Table 3.1 provides us with some useful data for illustrating the basic principles developed earlier in this chapter. First, past, or historical, costs have been ignored. The original costs of the part central heating system and the oil heaters have no bearing on the decision and do not enter into either Table 3.1 or Table 3.2.

Secondly, the payments to the local Gas Board for servicing and maintaining the central heating system do not affect the decision. The cash cost is the same whether or not the system is extended. This illustrates the principle that only differential costs need be considered. Table 3.1 also illustrates the central importance of cash flows in this sort of analysis. A final statement of costs and benefits may be in the form of a difference column or be presented along the lines of Table 3.2; underlying every figure in the final statement will be a comparison between two or more alternative cash flows. It will often be possible to enter figures directly in the difference column but where difficulty is encountered in calculating a particular cost, reference might usefully be made to the underlying alternative cash flows.

Consider the situation if Mr Frost, knowing and believing the figures in Tables 3.1 and 3.2, decides to proceed with the extension to his central heating system. The implication is that there are other, non-cash, benefits, not included in the original statements, which have influenced Mr Frost's decision. These might include the convenience of a fully automatic system, the increased heating efficiency compared with the present piecemeal arrangement and the status attached to full, rather than part, central heating. Insufficient information is provided to enable us to put a precise value on these factors (the easiest way would be to ask Mr Frost at how much he values them) but Mr Frost's behaviour implies that he values them at a figure of at least £110 over a period of three years, for this is the extra cost he is willing to incur to secure them.

In the above example, the timing of the cash flows has been ignored. It is not a main purpose of this text to consider the effects of introducing an interest rate into the calculations. But this element of the decision may be critical in some situations in practice and for this reason we shall extend the example and make use of the net present value decision rule developed in the previous chapter. Specifically, we shall calculate the incremental cost in present value terms of extending the central heating system if Mr Frost is able both to lend and borrow funds freely at 10%.

Table 3.3

Cash flow at end of year:	0	1	2	3
	£	£	£	£
Cost of extension	−200	0	0	0
Extra sales proceeds	0	0	0	+150
Extra fuel costs of full gas central heating	0	−70	−70	−70
Saving on running costs of oil heaters	0	+50	+50	+50
	−200	−20	−20	+130

On the assumption that the extension cost of £200 is payable immediately and that other cash flows will be received or paid on the last day of the year in which they fall due we may analyse the timing of the cash flows in the difference column of Table 3.1. The analysis is given in Table 3.3. The net present value of the extension is:

$$- 200 - \frac{20}{(1+i)} - \frac{20}{(1+i)^2} + \frac{130}{(1+i)^3}.$$

Substituting the relevant interest rate of 10% (or 0.1 as a decimal of 1) we get:

$$- 200 - \frac{20}{(1.1)} - \frac{20}{(1.1)^2} + \frac{130}{(1.1)^3} = - £137.$$

In present value terms, using a discount rate of 10%, the incremental cost of extending the central heating system is £137.

3.2   *The Concept of Opportunity Cost*
The principles developed so far in this chapter are not inconsistent

with the economist's concept of opportunity cost.[2] Cohen and Cyert,
for example, on the subject of opportunity costs say: 'Economists
define costs in terms of *alternative costs* or *opportunity costs*. The
alternative cost doctrine states that the cost of a productive factor is
the maximum value that this factor could produce in an alternative
use. An equivalent definition is that the cost of using a productive
factor to produce any commodity is the value of the best opportunity
which is foregone by not using this factor in another way.'[3] For the
purposes of our analysis it is convenient to separate opportunity cost
into two components; external opportunity cost and internal
opportunity cost.

External opportunity cost: The external opportunity cost of accepting a
particular opportunity may be defined as the difference between total
net cash outflows if the opportunity is accepted and those if it is
rejected. The change in net cash outflows of £110 that would have
been incurred by Mr Frost had he decided to extend his central
heating system falls into this particular category of opportunity cost.
In a normal business situation the external opportunity cost of a
particular course of action will often equal the total current buying
prices of the various input factors to be used.

Internal opportunity cost: The internal opportunity cost of a particular
course of action may be defined as the net benefits that will accrue to
the firm from its next best opportunities only if the particular course of
action is rejected. There are, broadly speaking, two situations in which
internal opportunity costs may arise. The first is where one or more of
the resources of the business is scarce. Scarce resources exist when a
firm has insufficient supplies of input factors to undertake all
opportunities that seem worthwhile when the inputs required are
valued at their external opportunity cost. In this situation, it may be

2. For articles by economists on the basic concept of opportunity cost see, for
   example, COASE, R H, 'The Nature of Costs', in SOLOMONS, D (ed),
   Studies in Cost Analysis, Sweet and Maxwell, 1968, and GOULD, J R, 'The
   Economist's Cost Concept and Business Problems', IN BAXTER, W T and
   DAVIDSON, S (eds), Studies in Accounting Theory, Sweet and Maxwell,
   1962.
3. COHEN, K J and CYERT, R M, Theory of the Firm: Resource Allocation
   in a Market Economy, Prentice-Hall, 1965, page 92.

necessary to value the scarce resources at something more than their external opportunity cost to reflect their relative scarcity. This problem is dealt with in Chapters 7 and 8.

The second situation in which internal opportunity costs may arise is where two or more of the opportunities under consideration are mutually exclusive, as in the example cited earlier (page 31) where a firm had decided to build a new factory and was considering what size

Table 3.4

	Production Process I £	*Production Process II* £
Contract price	5,000	5,000
Less External opportunity cost	2,500	3,000
Surplus on contract[4]	2,500	2,000

it should be. Let us consider another example of mutually exclusive projects. A firm has been offered a contract to manufacture 1,000 components type AD3 at a price of £5 per component. There are two production processes that it could use, neither of which requires any scarce resources, and details of the costs associated with each one are shown in Table 3.4. It is clear that on the basis of the figures in Table 3.4 the firm should accept the contract and manufacture the components using Production Process I which yields the greater surplus. A rigid application of the economist's concept of opportunity cost would include as a cost of Production Process I the surplus foregone by no longer being able to accept the contract using Production Process II. This surplus we shall call the internal opportunity cost of Production Process I. Thus the revised surplus under Production Process I is £(2,500 — 2,000) or £500. Similarly the revised surplus if the firm uses Production Process II is £(2,000—2,500)

---

4. The word 'surplus' is used intentionally here instead of 'profit' to avoid the confusion resulting from the variety of meanings commonly attached to the latter.

or $-£500$. The decision is the same; Production Process I is
profitable relative to Production Process II.

If we apply this concept of opportunity cost, where the total
opportunity cost of a particular course of action is given by the sum of
its external and internal opportunity costs, then our decision rule is to
accept those opportunities with a positive surplus and to reject those
whose surplus is negative. While this may at first sight seem a useful
advance on having to rank mutually exclusive alternatives it is, in
this context, somewhat redundant. In order to determine the internal
opportunity costs of the various alternatives we must first rank them
to ascertain which is the best alternative rejected in each case: we are
unable to calculate the internal opportunity costs until we know the
optimal plan, by which time they are unnecessary. The concept is of
limited use in choosing between mutually exclusive alternatives. At
this stage, however, it does serve to stress that decisions are concerned
with choices between alternatives and for that reason it should not be
ignored.

We have now compared our earlier framework of incremental
cash flow analysis with the economist's basic concept of opportunity
cost. We have yet to consider how this concept might be applied to a
situation of scarce resources. We shall now consider a further example
that is more complex than previous ones and illustrates the practical
application of some of the principles developed so far, while contrasting
our approach with that often advocated as traditional accounting
practice.

Example

Gunners Ltd manufactures scientific instruments. It is considering
whether to accept a contract to manufacture a batch of oscilloscopes.
The contract would last for 52 weeks. The following statement has been
prepared on the basis of which it is recommended that the contract
should not be accepted:

	£	£
Materials: A—already in stock (original cost)	750	
B—ordered (original contract price)	900	1,650

	£	£
Labour:		3,500
Machinery: Leased at £50 per week	2,600	
Already owned—depreciation	2,000	4,600
General overheads: 100% on labour		3,500
		13,250
Contract price offered:		10,000
Loss on contract:		3,250

The following additional information is available:

(1)   *Materials*: Material A was purchased two years ago at a cost of
£750. If sold now it would realise £500. Alternatively, it could
be adapted and used on another job as a substitute for material
presently costing £800. It would cost £150 to make the
necessary adaptation.

Material B was ordered 6 months ago when the price
was £900. Delivery has been delayed by a strike in the
supplier's factory and agreement has been reached between the
supplier and Gunners Ltd that a discount of £200 be allowed
against the original contract price to compensate for the delay.
If material B is not used on the oscilloscope contract the only
alternative is to sell it for £450.

(2)   *Labour*: The labour charge of £3,500 in the statement includes
£1,000 in respect of a foreman's wages. Unlike the rest of the
labour to be used on the contract, the foreman will be
employed whether or not it is accepted. However, if he does
have to work on the contract the company will have to
employ someone else at a wage of £15 per week to do the work
he could otherwise have done.

(3)   *Machinery*: Two machines will have to be used on the contract.
One is a machine the company is already leasing for £50 per
week. This machine is at present being used in another

department and if i⁺ is transferred for use on the oscilloscope
contract another machine will have to be leased for £28 per
week and additional labour costing £30 per week will have to
be hired to maintain production in the other department.

The second machine was purchased by the company
3 years ago for £10,000. Its estimated life was then 5 years at
the end of which time it was estimated that it would have no
scrap or re-sale value, and hence straight-line depreciation at the
rate of £2,000 per annum is being written off.[5] If it is not used
on this contract the machine will be sold immediately for
£2,500. Otherwise it will be sold after completion of the
contract for an estimated price of £1,200.

(4) *General overheads*: In past years general overheads, which include
such items as rent, rates and other administrative expenses,
have equalled approximately 100% of direct labour. Allowance
has been made for overhead costs at that rate. All expenses
included under this heading are expected to remain unchanged
whether or not the contract is accepted.

(5) The storage space that will be required if the job is undertaken
can be provided only if the construction of a new works canteen
is delayed for one year.

We are required to redraft the original statement, if we think it
necessary, and to advise Gunners Ltd whether to accept the contract.

5. The straight-line method of depreciation is widely used in practice. The
formula for calculating the annual depreciation charge under this method is:

$$D = \frac{C - S}{L}$$

where D is the annual depreciation
        C is the initial cost of the asset
        S is the estimated scrap or re-sale value of the asset at the
        end of its life
    and L is the estimated life, expressed in years.
So in the above example annual depreciation, D, is £(10,000 − 0)/5, which
equals £2,000.

One approach, consistent with the principles discussed so far, would be to enumerate all the alternatives available to Gunners Ltd and to prepare a cash budget for each of them, selecting the alternative with the largest cash surplus. Within the limitations of the framework, for example those imposed by the assumption of certainty and the irrelevance of the time factor, this should lead to a solution that may be demonstrated to be the best available. However, even in this relatively simple example there is a complicated combination of alternatives and a statement along the lines of Table 3.1 would require a large number of columns. Instead we shall endeavour to prepare a 'single column' statement as in Table 3.2 (which was based on the difference column of Table 3.1). Use will be made of 'extracts' from the implied alternative cash budgets to ascertain the relevant cost and benefit figures to be included in the statement. Each item to be included will be discussed separately prior to the preparation of the final statement.

Material A: The original cost of material A is the result of a previous decision and cannot be altered by any decision made now. It is therefore irrelevant. If the material is not used on the oscilloscope contract there appear to be two alternative uses for it. It could be sold immediately for £500 or it could be used as a substitute for another type of material. If the firm does not accept the oscilloscope contract to which of these alternative uses will it put material A? The first alternative would increase Gunners' cash resources by £500. The second would prevent a decrease of £800 in the cash fund (the amount saved by not having to purchase the material for which A is a substitute) but would give rise to a cash outflow of £150 (the adaptation cost), a net gain in cash terms of £650 on the assumption that there are no holding costs and the like, associated with keeping material A for future use, other than those already mentioned. Following an objective of maximising current cash resources, Gunners would choose the second alternative. In determining the relevant cost of material A for inclusion in the final statement, we may consider extracts from two cash budgets; using material A on the oscilloscope contract and using it as a substitute:

	(1) *Oscilloscope* *contract* £	(2) *Substitute* £	(1)–(2) *Difference* £
Cost of alternative material if contract accepted	−800	0	−800
Cost of adaptation if contract rejected	0	−150	+150
			−650

There is a negative cash difference of £650 if the contract is accepted which is the relevant cost of using material A on the contract.

Material B: The implication here seems to be that Gunners has a contractual obligation to purchase material B for £700. The original contract price is no longer relevant as it has subsequently been amended. Suppose first that the oscilloscope contract is rejected, what will the company do with material B? If the contract may be cancelled at no cost this would appear to be the best alternative, as far as material B is concerned; a saving of £700 is better in cash terms than a receipt of £450. But if the contract is legally binding and cannot be avoided, which is assumed to be the case here, the *only* course of action available if the oscilloscope contract is rejected is to sell material B for £450. It is worth noting that Gunners Ltd, if it rejects the oscilloscope contract, should be willing to pay up to £250 to avoid its legal obligation to buy material B for it will save that amount by so doing (a saving of £700 minus a loss of revenue of £450). Our assumption, however, is that the legal obligation cannot be avoided and the two uses of material B are reflected in the following alternative cash budget extract:

	(1) *Oscilloscope* *contract* £	(2) *Sell material* *B* £	(1)–(2) *Difference* £
Net purchase cost of material B	−700	−700	0

	£	£	£
Receipt from sale of material B	0	+450	−450
			−450

The purchase cost of material B is common to both alternatives and consequently is irrelevant for choosing between them. The only differential cash flow is the £450 which will be received if the oscilloscope contract is rejected. This is the relevant cost of using material B on the contract.

Labour: The charge for labour, other than the foreman, included in the original statement is £(3,500 − 1,000) which equals £2,500. If we assume that this labour may be hired for the duration of the contract and that £2,500 represents the full cash cost to the firm of employing it, then the alternative cash budget extracts will read:

	(1) *Accept contract* £	(2) *Reject contract* £	(1)–(2) *Difference* £
Cost of hiring labour	−2,500	0	−2,500

This negative cash flow of £2,500 represents the cost to Gunners Ltd of hiring labour, other than the foreman, for use on the contract.

Foreman: If the company accepts the contract it will have to pay the foreman £1,000. It will also have to employ someone else to replace him at a cost of £15 per week for 52 weeks, a total of £780. If Gunners rejects the contract it will still have to pay the foreman £1,000. The cash budget extract runs:

	(1) *Accept contract* £	(2) *Reject contract* £	(1)–(2) *Difference* £
Foreman's wages	−1,000	−1,000	0
Replacement's wages	− 780	0	−780
			−780

The foreman's wages of £1,000 are irrelevant as they are payable whether or not the contract is accepted. The cost of his replacement, however, is a relevant cost even though the replacement will be working in another department, as his wages represent an incremental cost to the firm of accepting the contract.

Leased machine: As with the foreman, the cost of the machine presently leased at £50 per week will be the same whether or not the contract is accepted (assuming that there are no costs involved in moving it from the other department). The cost of the replacement machine and labour, a total of £58 per week, will be incurred, however, only if the contract is accepted, a cost of £3,016(£58 × 52). The extract from the alternative budget statement will run:

	(1) *Accept contract* £	(2) *Reject contract* £	(1)–(2) *Difference* £
Cost of machine presently leased	−2,600	−2,600	0
Cost of replacement machine and labour	−3,016	0	−3,016
			−3,016

The relevant cost is the incremental cost incurred as a result of having to replace the machine presently leased so that it may be used on the oscilloscope contract, that is £3,016.

Owned machine: Strictly, depreciation may be defined as a fall in value. Conventionally accountants regard it as something rather different; they normally take it to mean some proportion of the cost of an asset written off in a particular period. In the case of Gunners Ltd the annual depreciation represents an amount, in this case constant each year, which is being written off the cost of the machine. The value pattern implied by the straight-line method of depreciation is linear as shown in Figure 3.1. W represents the initial cost of the machine and Z its value after 5 years (the end of its effective life). Annual

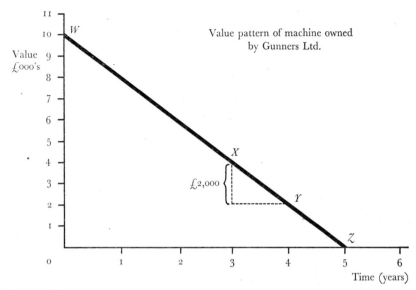

FIGURE 3.1

depreciation is constant each year at £2,000. The machine is to be used on the oscilloscope contract during the fourth year of its life when the straight-line depreciation method implies a fall in value from X to Y, that is from £4,000 to £2,000. But we are told that the re-sale value of the machine is £2,500 at the end of the third year of its life and £1,200 one year later and these values are relevant here as we are also told that Gunners Ltd intends to sell the machine now if the contract is rejected and in one year if it is accepted. A differential cash flow approach would produce the following figures:

	(1) *Accept* *contract* £	(2) *Reject* *contract* £	(1)–(2) *Difference* £
Receipt from selling machine now	0	+2,500	−2,500
Receipt from selling machine after one year	+1,200	0	+1,200
			−1,300

Following our earlier principles, this negative difference figure of
£1,300 represents the cost to Gunners Ltd of using this machine on the
contract. It depends on the information that the machine will be sold
as soon as possible; if the machine is to be retained for further use in
the firm the relevant values may be different. This is discussed further
later in this chapter (pages 51–53).

General overheads: In this case general overhead expenses will remain
unchanged whether or not the oscilloscope contract is accepted. If we
assume that these expenses are expected to amount to £X in the
coming year the alternative cash budget extract for the oscilloscope
contract will read:

	(1) *Accept* *contract* £	(2) *Reject* *contract* £	(1)–(2) *Difference* £
General overhead expenses	$-X$	$-X$	0 =

Whatever the level of general overhead expenses they are not relevant
to the decision on the oscilloscope contract and should not be included
in the final statement. Whether or not a particular cost is fixed will
depend on the circumstances obtaining. For example, consider a firm
renting a factory at an annual rental of £10,000 which is avoidable if
the firm vacates possession of the factory. If the decision is whether to
produce product A or product B in the factory the rent is irrelevant;
it is payable whichever alternative is selected. If, on the other hand, the
decision is whether to produce product A or product B or to produce
neither and vacate the factory then the rent is relevant as it may be
avoided if the third alternative is chosen. Accountants, however,
argue sometimes that fixed costs must be recovered and for that reason
allocate them to particular jobs or departments. It is true enough that
fixed costs must be covered if the firm is to avoid bankruptcy. It does
not follow that the best way to achieve this is to reject opportunities
that do not fully cover fixed costs allocated to them on a basis that
might imply that they are, in fact, avoidable. The problem of fixed
costs is considered further in Chapter 4.

Contract price: The contract price presents no particular problems. A differential cash flow statement reveals, as expected, that the relevant figure for inclusion in the final statement is £10,000:

	(1) Accept contract £	(2) Reject contract £	(1)–(2) Difference £
Proceeds from contract	+10,000	0	+10,000

Bearing in mind that we have not yet discussed the storage space that will be required if the contract is accepted, we may now proceed to prepare an amended statement for the oscilloscope contract.

Gunners Ltd   *Redrafted Statement—Oscilloscope Contract*

		£	£
Materials: A		650	
B		450	
		——	1,100
Labour:	Other than foreman	2,500	
	Replacement for foreman	780	
		——	3,280
Machinery:	Replacement for leased machine	3,016	
	Already owned	1,300	
		——	4,316
General overheads			0
			8,696
Contract price offered			10,000
Surplus on contract			1,304

The redrafted statement suggests that the contract should be accepted as it provides a positive surplus which may be used to pay some of the

fixed costs of the business. However, we must consider the possible
effects of delaying construction of the new works canteen for one year.
This delay may increase the probability of strike action by the work
force, increase demands for higher wages, decrease efficiency due to
longer lunch, coffee and tea breaks and so on. We have insufficient
information to attempt to quantify these possible effects. In any case
this quantification will probably have to be the subject of qualitative
judgement by management. If management should decide to reject the
contract we may at least reason, on the basis of the redrafted statement,
that they put the cost of delaying construction of the canteen at at
least £1,304; indeed, what they have to decide is whether the benefit
involved in having the canteen for an extra year is more or less than
£1,304.

3.3   A Comparison with the Conventional Accounting Approach

A number of areas of difference between the approach to decisions
recommended here and that resulting from the application of standard
accounting conventions are illustrated in the example of Gunners Ltd.
The first concerns the treatment of past costs.[6] The application of
accounting conventions may involve charging resources to particular
projects at their original cost, even where this has already been paid.
In support of this procedure, one might argue that if the value of the
resource has fallen (or risen) since purchase, the loss (or profit) must
be taken into account; but if the value has changed the consequent
loss (or profit) has already occurred regardless of any decision to be
made now and should not be added to (or subtracted from) the costs
of the opportunity under consideration. It is the alternative future uses
of the resource that must be considered, and the question to be
answered is what is the value of the resource in these alternative uses?
If the resource is one that is in regular use in the firm and its application
to a particular project will result merely in the firm having to
buy another for the alternative (i.e. to replace it), then the incremental
cost to the firm (the value in the alternative use) is the cost of

6. Alternatively described in the literature as historical costs or sunk costs.

replacement avoided. If, on the other hand, the alternative to use on a particular job is selling the resource, then the relevant cost of using it is the sale proceeds foregone by so doing, as was the case with material B in the example of Gunners Ltd. A third possibility arises when the factor is in short supply and this will be considered further in Chapters 7 and 8.

The second area of difference concerns fixed costs. Costs that are fixed regardless of the decision under consideration are not relevant costs of that decision for they cannot be affected by it. Nevertheless, in conventional accounting practice, fixed costs are often allocated to available opportunities.

The third major area of difference illustrated by Gunners Ltd is the treatment of depreciation of assets. The straight-line method of depreciation has already been mentioned. It is widely used in the reporting of financial information. There are a number of other methods, for example, the fixed percentage of reducing balance, sum-of-the-digits and annuity methods, most of which have one common characteristic: the annual depreciation charge can be calculated at the time of buying on the basis of the purchase price; any unexpected change in the value of the asset is usually brought into account, by means of a profit or loss on realisation, only when the asset is eventually disposed of. For short term decisions we need to know the sacrifice involved in using the asset on the particular project under consideration. There is no obvious reason why this should correspond to the writing off of original cost that typifies the traditional accounting concept of depreciation.

In the example of Gunners Ltd it was assumed that the firm would sell its machine immediately or after completion of the contract depending on whether the contract was accepted. In that situation it was demonstrated that the cost to the firm of using the machine on the contract was £1,300. Had a perfect market existed for the machines, in which the current value for three year old machines was £2,500 and that for four year old machines £1,200, the depreciation charge relevant for the contract would have been the same. If it had rejected the contract, the firm could have sold the machine immediately for £2,500 and purchased a similar four year old one after a year for £1,200, giving rise to the following differential cash flow statement:

	(1) Accept contract	(2) Reject contract	(1)–(2) Difference
	£	£	£
Sale of machine now	0	+2,500	−2,500
Purchase of machine after one year	0	−1,200	+1,200
			−1,300

It is perhaps unlikely that a decision on one contract would normally influence a firm's decision as to whether it should sell or retain a particular asset. Let us suppose that Gunners Ltd has decided to keep the machine for the next year whether or not it undertakes the oscilloscope contract. In this situation, it is useful to distinguish between the two main causes of depreciation; loss of value as a result of the passage of time and loss of value through use, sometimes called the user cost.[7] The former will arise whether or not the asset is used and, like other fixed costs, is irrelevant for short term decisions. The user cost, on the other hand, is a direct result of adopting a particular course of action, and must be taken into account. In the example of Gunners Ltd, if the value of the machine in one year is estimated at £1,200 if it is used on the contract and £1,500 if it is not, and the machine would be retained whether it was used or not, we may separate the depreciation as follows:

	£
Value now	2,500
Value after one year if not used	1,500
Time depreciation	1,000
Value after one year if not used	1,500
Value after one year if used	1,200
User depreciation (user cost)	300

In this situation the differential cash flow statement will read:

	(1) Accept contract £	(2) Reject contract £	(1)–(2) Difference £
Potential cash proceeds from selling machine at end of one year[8]	+1,200	+1,500	−300

The relevant cost of using the machine on the oscilloscope contract would be the user cost of £300.[9]

We have now developed some basic principles of cost evaluation from the valuation model and decision rule outlined in Chapter 2. A number of examples have been used to illustrate the practical application of these principles. The differences between the suggested approach and the approach implied by accounting conventions should not necessarily be interpreted as a criticism of traditional accounting. We saw in Chapter 2 that the information the accountant is expected to supply is, in practice, often used for a number of purposes including dividend determination, ascertainment of tax liability and control over certain of the stewardship duties of those responsible for running the firm. It does not follow that the same information will be useful for

---

7. In practice almost all assets fall in value due to the combined effect of time and use. An example of an asset normally depreciating solely because of the passage of time is a lease. It is less easy to find an asset whose value falls only when it is used; a freehold mine or quarry may suffice as an approximation.

8. The possibility of selling the machine immediately is precluded by our assumption that Gunners Ltd has decided to keep the machine for the coming year whether or not the contract is accepted.

9. A more detailed study of depreciation is outside the scope of this text. Fuller treatments may be found in BAXTER, W T, Depreciation, Sweet and Maxwell, 1971, and EDWARDS, E D and BELL, P W, The Theory and Measurement of Business Income, University of California Press, 1967, Chapter VI.

decision making purposes. Nevertheless, it is as well for the decision maker to be familiar with accounting conventions, for the data provided by the accountant are often the main source of information available to him.

4 Cost Behaviour

4.1 Patterns of Cost Behaviour

In the previous chapter we considered some basic principles of cost evaluation; this is the first step in estimating the various cost functions confronting the firm.[1] The same principles apply in estimating revenue functions. However the firm will not be able to derive an optimal plan by analysing the cost and revenue functions in isolation of each other no matter how refined the analysis might be. The solution depends on the movement of the cost and revenue functions relative to each other as a result of changes in output.[2] Factors other than output level changes may influence the level of costs and revenues; for example, changes in methods of production, changes in taste leading to changes in demand and so on. At present we are primarily concerned with selecting the output level that best satisfies the firm's objectives and consequently we are interested in changes to costs and revenues as a result of changes in output. For this purpose decisions about output

1. A function is an expression describing the behaviour of some variable (e.g. total cost) as the value of some other variable or variables (e.g. output) changes.
2. To simplify the exposition it will be assumed at this stage that stock levels do not change. Hence the amount produced (the output) is equal to the amount expected to be sold.

levels include the 'one-off' decision where a particular opportunity must be accepted or rejected. In such a case, only two output levels are possible: the level associated with acceptance and a zero level.

Before we consider the inter-relation of cost and revenue, we shall develop further our study of cost ascertainment by considering possible types of expected future cost behaviour; that is, the way in which costs might respond to changes in production volumes. This is important as we need to estimate total costs at various output levels if we are to ascertain the optimal level. Some costs may not respond at all to changes in volume. These are normally categorised as fixed costs. Other costs may respond in different ways. Many accountants assume, maybe for the sake of simplicity, that costs fall into one of two classes; either they are fixed in total regardless of the level of output or they vary proportionately with output. This basic dichotomy is useful but may be an over-simplification in some situations. We shall adopt a broader classification, distinguishing four basic categories of cost behaviour.

Two caveats will be issued before these categories are discussed in detail. First, the classification of a cost into a particular category will depend, amongst other things, on the decision to be made and, in particular, on the time period involved. A cost that is fixed for one decision may not be fixed for another (see, for example, page 48) and a cost that is regarded as fixed for one time period may not be fixed for a longer one.[3] Secondly, to preserve practicability in the analysis, costs are classified according to their behaviour within certain relevant ranges of output. For example, if a cost is expected to remain at the same level for all likely output levels it is classified as a fixed cost even if its behaviour at extreme, and unlikely, output levels fails to conform to this pattern. The four categories to be considered are variable costs, step variable costs, fixed costs and semi-variable costs.

3. The economist defines the long run as the period over which all costs may be varied. For example, Lipsey defines the short run as 'the period of time over which the inputs of some factors cannot be varied' and the long run as 'the period long enough for the inputs of all factors of production to be varied, but not so long that the basic technology of production changes', LIPSEY R G, An Introduction to Positive Economics, Weidenfeld and Nicolson, 1966, 2nd Edition, page 266.

Variable Costs: A particular cost is regarded as being variable if the level of the cost is expected to vary as a function of the level of output. Examples of such costs might be raw materials, manufacturing labour, commission on sales, power, carriage and certain clerical costs relating to sales. We may distinguish between two basic types of variable cost; those that vary linearly with output and those that vary in a curvilinear fashion with output.

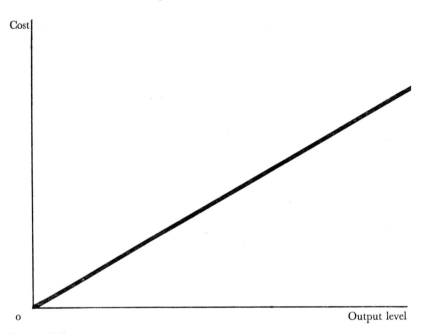

FIGURE 4.1

Figure 4.1 illustrates the linear behaviour expected of the first type of variable cost. It may be described by the general first degree equation $y = bx$, where y is the expected total cost for the particular item of expenditure, x is the expected level of output and b is a constant, the variable cost per unit. Suppose, for example, that a firm is manufacturing wallets and that each wallet requires one leather hide, each hide costing 25p. Then the cost per wallet, b in our equation, will equal £0.25. If the expected production of wallets in the coming year, x in our equation, is 50,000 then the total cost of leather hides in the

coming year will be $y = £(0.25 \times 50,000)$ which is £12,500.
Accountants normally assume that all variable costs are of this type,
varying in a linear fashion with output. Within certain relevant ranges
of output the assumed linearity may give a sufficiently close
approximation of the actual function to avoid the necessity of the
more complex calculations associated with curvilinear functions.

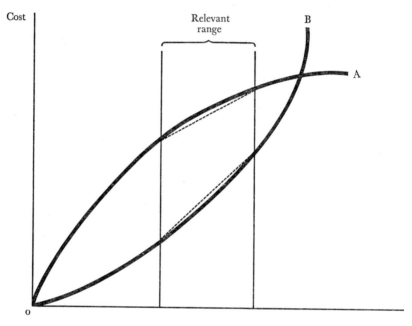

FIGURE 4.2

A cost that varies in a curvilinear fashion with output may be
described by a general equation of more than one degree, for example
a quadratic equation, $y = ax + bx^2$, a cubic equation, $y = ax + bx^2 +
cx^3$, or more generally an equation of the nth degree, $y = ax + bx^2 + cx^3
+ \ldots \ldots + px^n$, where y is again the expected total cost for the
particular item, x is the expected output and $a, b, c, \ldots \ldots, p$ are
constants. Two examples of cost functions that may be described by
quadratic equations are shown in Figure 4.2. In the case of curve A,
an extra unit of output leads to a less than proportional increase in

cost. For curve B, cost increases more than proportionately (i.e., the cost of extra units increases) as output increases. The broken lines indicate the linear functions that might be used as approximations of the original curves. For the remainder of this chapter it will be assumed that variable cost functions may be described or at least sufficiently approximated by linear equations.[4]

Step variable costs: Input factors that cannot be increased in infinitely small doses give rise to step cost functions: the input factor can be increased only in discrete 'lumps'. Strictly, nearly all variable costs fall into this category but often the steps are sufficiently shallow and frequent for a continuous curve to serve as an adequate approximation. However, consider, for example, the case of workshop quality control supervisors. If the firm decides that the maximum number of units any one supervisor should inspect in a week is 500 and it pays each supervisor £30 a week the expected supervisor cost-volume relationship will be as shown in Figure 4.3. In this case the steps are probably too deep and infrequent for the cost function to be approximated by a straight line.

If the relevant range of possible outputs being considered by the firm lies all within one step (for example, if the output level must, for other reasons, be between 2,001 and 2,500 units a week) the supervisor cost may be treated as a fixed cost (of £150 per week). If not, it will be necessary to calculate the cost of supervisors separately for various projected output levels.

There is no simple algebraic expression to describe step functions, but they may be added to other cost functions on a graph to determine a total cost function by calculating total cost at each level of output. As noted above, if the step function is represented by numerous small steps, it may be adequately approximated by a linear

4. It should be noted that the variable costs discussed here are not synonymous with the direct costs of the accountant. For example, Horngren describes direct labour as '. . . all labour which is obviously related to and easily traceable to a specific product . . .', HORNGREN, C T, Accounting for Management Control—An Introduction, Prentice-Hall, 1970, 2nd Edition, page 235. Our concept of variable cost corresponds closely with the economist's definition of marginal cost, the increase in total cost if one extra unit of output is produced.

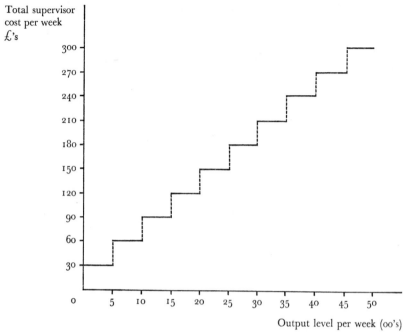

Total supervisor cost per week £'s

FIGURE 4.3

curve. In the variable cost example of the leather hides in the previous section, if the requirement for each wallet was, in fact, 1/4 of a hide and each hide cost £1.00 (the same average cost per wallet of 25p) the cost-volume relationship for the first 50 wallets would be as shown in Figure 4.4. The original linear variable curve is also shown and may serve as an adequate approximation of the step function bearing in mind that Figure 4.4 is an extract from a much larger graph whose x-axis will probably exceed 50,000 units and whose y-axis will consequently exceed £12,500. On the full graph the step function would be barely discernible from the straight line.

Fixed costs: Fixed costs are costs that are expected to remain unchanged whatever output level is chosen, or whatever the outcome of the decision being considered. A fixed cost is described by the general expression $y = a$, where y is the expected total cost for the particular item of expenditure and a is a constant. It should be noted that x, the

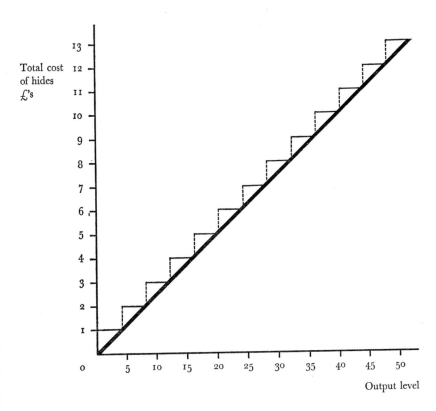

FIGURE 4.4

decision variable, does not affect the level of fixed costs. This is consistent with our earlier conclusion that costs that are not expected to vary consequent on a particular decision are not relevant to it. Strictly, according to our definition, all fixed costs are of the sort illustrated in Figure 4.5, where the level of cost is constant at all volumes including a zero volume. In practice, many items normally categorised as fixed costs, for example rent, rates, certain administrative salaries and clerical expenses, may be avoidable if nothing is produced. These will be characterised by the sort of cost function shown in Figure 4.6.

For the purposes of our analysis of optimal output levels we shall assume that all fixed costs fall into the first category; that is we shall

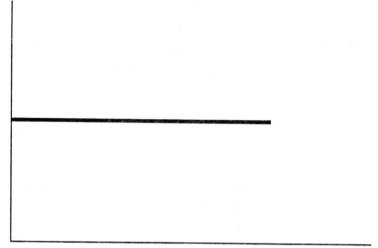

FIGURE 4.5

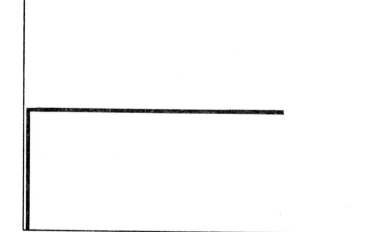

FIGURE 4.6

presume that the temporary or permanent closure of the business would require separate and special consideration.

Semi-variable costs: Many costs have both a fixed and a variable element. These are normally known as semi-variable costs, or mixed costs, and are characterised by the type of cost-volume relationship shown in Figure 4.7. An example might be a factory maintenance

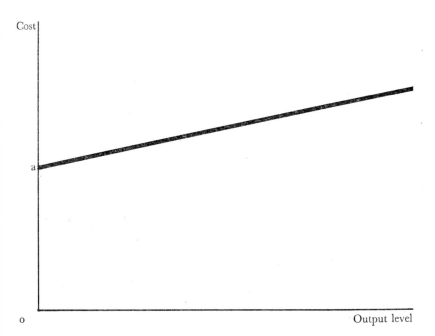

FIGURE 4.7

department requiring certain basic equipment and labour (represented by, say, *oa* in Figure 4.7) and also incurring variable costs as the level of activity required of it increases. That part of the function representing the variable cost of the particular factor need not be linear. Like wholly variable costs it might have to be described by a curvilinear function. If the total factor cost has a variable element that is linear it may be described by the general linear equation $y = a + bx$, where y is the expected total factor cost, x is the expected level of output and a and b are constants, b representing the variable cost per additional unit of output and a the fixed element of the total cost which will be incurred at all levels of output.

The cost-volume relationship of a semi-variable cost whose variable element is not linear may be described by a general equation of the nth degree, $y = a + bx + cx^2 + \ldots + px^n$, where y and x are defined as previously and $a, b, c, \ldots, p$ are constants, a representing

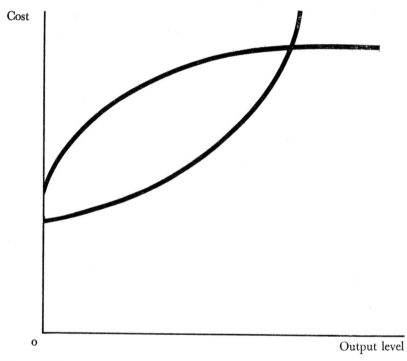

Cost

o

Output level

FIGURE 4.8

the fixed element of the cost. Examples of semi-variable cost functions that may be described by second degree equations are given in Figure 4.8. As was the case with wholly variable costs it will be assumed for the rest of this chapter that the variable part of semi-variable cost functions may be described or at least sufficiently approximated by linear equations.

The four categories discussed above are presented as guidelines of the ways in which costs might behave. Few costs will conform exactly to one of the patterns mentioned but in many cases the divergence will be small enough for the general functions outlined above to be sufficiently accurate approximations. We shall consider in Chapter 5 how firms might utilise past cost data to estimate the level of future costs. First we shall examine further some of the ways in which fixed costs are treated in practice and suggest an alternative approach more consistent with the assumed behaviour of such costs.

4.2 Fixed Costs and the Contribution Approach

It was mentioned in Chapter 3 that accountants often prepare profit statements in which fixed costs are allocated between departments or opportunities, on the grounds that fixed costs must be recovered if the firm is to avoid bankruptcy. Is this method of cost calculation, normally called absorption costing, likely to lead the firm to a plan that may be demonstrated to be optimal in terms of the firm's assumed objective of maximising its current cash inflows?

Consider the example of a firm that has three departments, A, B and C, each manufacturing and selling a separate product and all operating in the same factory building. The firm's book-keeper has prepared the statement shown in Table 4.1 which shows the results expected in the coming year. On the basis of the profit and loss figures in the statement he recommends that Department C should be closed

Table 4.1

	Total £000's	Dept. A £000's	Dept. B £000's	Dept. C £000's
Sales		370	100	200	70
Variable costs	270	60	150	60
Fixed costs:				
Rent and rates	28	10	5	13
Other overheads	37	10	20	7
Total costs	335	80	175	80
Net profit/(loss)	35	20	25	(10)

down during the coming year. Sales are attributed to the departments on the basis of the quantities of the products each department is expected to manufacture and sell. The firm is not faced with a scarcity of resources and the variable costs have been calculated for each department on an external opportunity cost basis (see Chapter 2). Fixed costs are expected to remain at £65,000 whatever decision is

Table 4.2

		Dept. C open £000's		*Dept. C closed* £000's
Sales		370		300
Variable costs	270		210	
Fixed costs	65		65	
	—		—	
Total costs		335		275
Net profit		35		25

taken concerning Department C but the book-keeper has endeavoured to recover them from the departments, arguing that 'each department should bear its fair share of the cost of the resources it uses'. Two bases have been used for recovering fixed costs. Rent and rates have been charged according to the amount of floor space occupied by each department and other fixed overheads have been recovered on the basis of expected turnover.

   Table 4.2 shows the total expected 'profit' position of the firm ('profit' here being assumed to correspond with cash surplus) if Department C is kept open and if it is closed down. It is clear from the table that the firm will be £10,000 worse off if the department is closed. By closing Department C the firm will lose the sales revenue it would have produced (£70,000) and save the variable costs it would have incurred (£60,000), a net loss of £10,000. It will not avoid any of the fixed costs that the book-keeper has allocated to the department, nor, it is assumed, can it offset the loss by subletting the space.

   How might the book-keeper have formulated his statement in Table 4.1 to reflect the crucial difference between variable and fixed costs? In Chapter 3 (pages 32–34) we developed basic principles of cost (and revenue) evaluation which suggested that only expected future cash flows that will differ under the alternatives available should be considered. If we apply these principles to the information in Table 4.1 we might construct the statement shown in Table 4.3.

Table 4.3

	Total £000's	Dept. A £000's	Dept. B £000's	Dept. C £000's
Sales	370	100	200	70
Variable costs	270	60	150	60
Contribution to fixed costs and profit	100	40	50	10
Fixed costs	65			
Net profit	35			

The relevant figure for assessing the worthwhileness of a particular department is the contribution it makes to the fixed costs and profit of the firm; that is, the difference between the incremental revenues and the incremental costs of each department. As the contribution measures the difference between incremental revenues and incremental costs the firm that maximises total contribution will have the largest possible surplus from which to pay its (unavoidable) fixed costs.

Allocating fixed costs on any basis is confusing and may lead to those costs being treated as though they were variable and accordingly to the rejection of opportunities that may improve the cash position of the firm. It is accepted that fixed costs must be recovered. But the best way of recovering them may not be by allocation but by a policy of accepting projects that cover and more than cover their associated incremental costs. This should ensure that the firm achieves the largest possible surplus or contribution from which to pay fixed costs. The contribution approach will play an important part in our subsequent examination of investment opportunities.

4.3   A Further Example of the Contribution Approach

This chapter has been concerned primarily with differing patterns of cost behaviour and the different treatment appropriate to each pattern. A further example should stress the usefulness of the contribution approach in distinguishing fixed and variable elements of cost and in avoiding the confusion that may arise if fixed costs are allocated.

The Flaxmin Motor Co Ltd recently suffered a strike that lasted for two weeks. During that time no motor cars were produced. The company issued a press statement to the effect that the cost of the strike was £500,000. This figure was estimated on the basis of lost production of 1,000 vehicles, each of which could have been sold for £500, a total loss of turnover of £500,000. The company's accountant feels that this figure over-states the cost of the strike and produces the following statement to support his view:

Expenses avoided:	£
Materials (£100 per car)	100,000
Production labour (£50 per car)	50,000
Depreciation of machinery	175,000
Overheads: 200% on production labour	100,000
	425,000
Loss of sales revenue:	500,000
Cost of strike:	75,000

The following additional information is available:

(1)   Depreciation of machinery is based on the straight-line method of calculation (see page 42). However, the plant manager estimates that the machinery will fall in value by £20,000 each week regardless of the level of production. He feels that, in

addition, its value will fall by £15,000 for every 100 cars that
are produced.[5]

(2) Overhead expenses are recovered at the rate of 200% on
production labour. Most of the overhead expenses are
unaffected by the level of production, for example rent, rates,
maintenance and staff wages, but some, such as power and
lighting, vary directly with production. The general manager
estimates that the latter type of overhead expense amounts to
£1,000 for every 100 cars produced.

(3) During the period of the strike the maintenance staff, whose
wages are included in the fixed overhead expense, carried out a
major overhaul on one of the company's machines using
materials costing £1,000. This overhaul would normally have
been performed by an outside contractor at a price, including
materials, of £10,000.

(4) The sales manager feels that about one half of the production
lost could be made up and sold in the next month by the
production labour working overtime. Labour is paid at the rate
of time and one half for overtime working.

We must decide whether the original press statement or the
accountant's revised statement properly reflect the cost of the strike to
Flaxmin Motor Co Ltd.

First consider the contribution lost by the company as a result
of the strike ignoring, at present, the possibility of recouping some of
the lost sales in the ensuing month. The contribution the company
would have earned during the two week period comprises the sales
revenue it would have received less the variable (or external
opportunity) costs it would have incurred. The sales revenue would
have been 1,000 vehicles at £500 each or £500,000. The variable costs
would have included materials and production labour, assuming that
no production would mean no cost being incurred in respect of either
of these factors. The material cost would have been £100,000
(1,000 × £100) and the production labour cost £50,000 (1,000 ×
£50).

5. In practice, this type of information may be hard to get. The example
illustrates the data which are required rather than how to obtain them.

Both depreciation and overheads fall into the category of semi-variable costs. To calculate the contribution lost we need to consider only the variable part of such costs, the fixed part would have been incurred in any case. The depreciation figure included in the accountant's statement is no more than a writing off of historical cost and does not represent an opportunity cost. Assuming that the machinery was not sold at the beginning of the strike the fall in value of £20,000 per week would have occurred whether or not production had continued. For the purposes of ascertaining the cost of the strike it is a fixed cost and hence irrelevant. However, the fall in value which would have occurred had the machines been used (the user cost) is a variable cost amounting to £150,000 (1,000/100 × £15,000) and is relevant.

Those overheads that are fixed regardless of the level of production may be ignored as they would have been payable with or without the strike. The recovery of overheads at 200% of production labour is not relevant for our purposes as it does not represent an external opportunity cost. Only the overheads which have been avoided as a result of the strike should be included—that is, £10,000 (1,000/100 × £1,000).

We may now draw up a preliminary statement of the contribution lost as a result of the strike:

	£	£
Sales revenue		500,000
Less Materials	100,000	
Production labour	50,000	
Fall in value of machinery	150,000	
Variable overheads	10,000	
		310,000
Contribution lost		190,000

This is still not the full picture. By utilising the maintenance staff to carry out the major overhaul the company paid only for materials (£1,000). An outside contractor would have charged £10,000. A saving of £9,000 has been effected which would not have been possible without the strike. In addition, the sales manager feels that about one half of the lost production could be made up and sold next month. The contribution from these sales is a result of the strike and consequently should be deducted from its cost. The extra contribution will be:

	£	£
Sales revenue (500 cars)		250,000
Less Materials	50,000	
Production labour (at time and a half)	37,500	
Fall in value of machinery	75,000	
Variable overheads	5,000	167,500
Contribution		82,500

The final statement of the net cost of the strike to Flaxmin Motor Co Ltd might read:

	£	£
Contribution lost during strike period		190,000
Less Saving on overhaul	9,000	
Increased contribution expected next month	82,500	91,500
Cost of strike		98,500

On the basis of the information given it seems that neither the press statement nor the statement of the accountant properly reflects the loss resulting from the strike. Even now a number of assumptions that are implicit in the calculations may not be valid. Was the major overhaul really necessary? Is machine capacity adequate to make up one half of the lost production next month? Will the market buy the extra production *and* the normal monthly production next month at the prices assumed? What interest costs are involved in delaying some production for one month? Is there likely to be any permanent effect on customer goodwill as a result of the increased waiting list for the company's motor cars? These and other points must be considered. They highlight once again the need for value judgements by management. The methodology suggested is designed to supplement management expertise, not to replace it.

5 Cost Estimation

5.1 The Prediction of Costs

In the previous chapter we discussed the varying behaviour patterns we might expect costs to follow. We shall consider now some of the means available for estimating the level of future costs given some level of output. One way is to ask those responsible for certain areas of the firm's business to make direct estimates of the costs expected in those areas. Their answers will probably be based on their experience of cost levels in the past plus any knowledge they may have of environmental changes likely to affect the future level of costs. We may be able to make the task easier by formalising this intuitive process and deriving a model to predict future cost levels from historical data, particularly as most firms have a wealth of such data available. The usefulness of such a methodology will depend on the existence in the future of circumstances similar to those which have obtained in the past subject to adjustments being made for any foreseeable changes.

Our discussion so far has, for ease of exposition, assumed that cost behaviour is linked to variations in output. Similarly our investigation of predictive methods will be based on the assumption that the variability of future costs will depend mainly on output. This assumption may not always be apposite or at least sufficiently appropriate for the resultant predictions to be useful. If so, an

alternative model may need to be constructed, incorporating other
variables to predict future cost levels. The means available for
determining the adequacy of a particular model will be discussed later
when a detailed example is considered.

5.2 Statistical Cost Estimation: Linear Regression

There are a number of relatively rough and ready methods that might
be used to predict future costs from historical data.[1] These tend to be
less rigorous and consistent than well-tried statistical techniques. It is
not within the scope of this text to examine all the statistical methods
that might be applied to predicting future costs. We shall simplify
matters by retaining the assumption we made in discussing cost
behaviour, that cost functions are of the general form[2] $y = a + bx$.
Statistical techniques are available for dealing with non-linear
functions and numerous variables but a linear function is simpler to
handle and may often be a sufficiently accurate approximation of real
world conditions to serve the purposes of the decision maker.

Basically, the problem is one of linear curve fitting (i.e. finding
the straight line that fits the available data best). Certain historical
data are available about cost levels at differing output levels and, on
the assumption of an unchanged environment, we wish to derive a
linear function to predict the level of costs at other levels of output.
One statistical technique available for solving this problem is known as
linear regression.[3]

It may be helpful to make use of an example to illustrate the
principle and technique of linear regression. Before we do so, two
further points should be mentioned. First, the input data (past costs)

---

1. For examples see DOPUCH, N and BIRNBERG, J G, Cost Accounting:
   Accounting Data for Management's Decisions, Harcourt, Brace & World,
   1969, pages 47–53, and HORNGREN, C T, Accounting for Management
   Control: An Introduction, Prentice-Hall, 1970—2nd Edition, pages 242–245.
2. In the case of variable costs, a assumes a zero value and in the case of
   fixed costs b is defined to be zero.
3. A more detailed explanation of linear regression than is given here may be
   found in most basic statistics texts. The formulas used here are taken from
   FREUND, J E and WILLIAMS, F J, Modern Business Statistics, Sir Isaac
   Pitman and Sons Ltd, 1959, chapters 13 and 14.

that are used should be adjusted to current buying prices; unamended accounting data may produce estimates of future costs inconsistent with those required for our decision model. Secondly, we note that linear regression analysis may be applied to individual items or categories of cost, cost functions of departments or divisions, or the total cost function of the firm. The most common application is probably the first of these and the following example is of this kind.

Example
Jacobin Ltd manufactures a single product. In order to decide how many units of the product it should manufacture in the coming year (19x7) it wishes to estimate the total level of costs at various levels of output. The company incurs three basic types of cost: variable (linear) costs, fixed costs and semi-variable costs. It predicts that the variable costs will be £6.40 per unit of output and the fixed costs £5,850.00 for the coming year. It is unsure about how to predict the level of semi-variable costs. The following data are available, concerning the level of semi-variable costs in the previous six years:

Year	Output Units	Total semi-variable costs £
19x1	1,748	6,314
19x2	1,525	5,630
19x3	2,036	6,628
19x4	2,240	7,880
19x5	1,981	6,762
19x6	2,175	7,245

All costs have been adjusted to current price levels. No changes in the efficiency of operations have taken place within the past six years, nor are any expected during the coming year. The problem is to derive a functional relationship to predict the level of semi-variable costs (y) dependent upon the level of output (x).

The six points given by the above data are plotted on the graph in Figure 5.1. If we are to use these historical data to predict the level of semi-variable costs in the coming year we need to establish the

equation of the line which in some sense provides the best fit to these
points. At this stage our assumption is that the equation is linear. The
validity of this assumption will be tested later. One possibility is to fit
the line visually, that is to draw the straight line that appears to fit

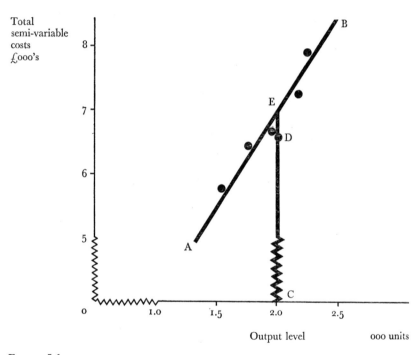

FIGURE 5.1

the plotted data best. There are two problems with this method. First,
it is likely that different people will fit different lines to the same set
of data, and there is no obvious criterion for choosing which is the best
fit. Second, the method lacks objectivity and makes the evaluation of
predictions made from the assumed equation difficult. For these
reasons we shall utilise the best known statistical method of linear curve
fitting, the method of least squares. This requires that the line that we
fit is such that the sum of the squares of the vertical differences
between the observed data and the points predicted by the line at the

same output levels is minimised.[4] For example, point D on the graph in Figure 5.1 represents an observed cost of £6,628 (CD) at an output level of 2,036 units (for 19x3). If line AB is to be tested for fit, we first calculate the cost predicted by that line at the same output level; the predicted cost is CE. The difference between the observed and predicted cost at the output level is DE. Similarly, we could calculate the difference between actual and predicted cost for each other output level observed between 19 × 1 and 19 × 6. To find the 'sum of the squares', we square each difference and add the resulting figures.

We could follow this procedure for all lines that might fit the data. We choose the line that gives the lowest value to the 'sum of the squares' calculation. We shall describe the line of best fit by the equation $y' = a + bx$. To determine this equation by trial and error would be very time-consuming. Fortunately, there are formulas for calculating the values of a and b in the equation. They are:

$$a = \frac{\sum_{i=1}^{n} y_i - b . \sum_{i=1}^{n} x_i}{n}$$

$$b = \frac{n \left(\sum_{i=1}^{n} x_i y_i \right) - \left(\sum_{i=1}^{n} x_i \right) \left(\sum_{i=1}^{n} y_i \right)}{n \left(\sum_{i=1}^{n} x_i^2 \right) - \left(\sum_{i=1}^{n} x_i \right)^2} .$$

In these formulas, x_i is the observed output in year i, y_i is the observed level of semi-variable costs in year i and n is the number of observations. The formulas look imposing, but by arranging the data as in Table 5.1 the necessary figures are easily extracted. We first calculate the value of b which is then substituted into the first equation to determine the value of a. The calculations are tedious if performed manually, but relatively swift if electronic computers or calculating machines are

4. For an explanation as to why the *squares* of the differences are minimised and for a statement of the formulas used for calculating a and b see FREUND, J E and WILLIAMS, F J, Modern Business Statistics, Sir Isaac Pitman and Sons Ltd, 1959, pages 290–292.

Table 5.1

Year	Output x_i Units	Semi-variable cost y_i £	x_i^2	$x_i y_i$
19x1	1,748	6,314	3,055,504	11,036,872
19x2	1,525	5,630	2,325,625	8,585,750
19x3	2,036	6,628	4,145,296	13,494,608
19x4	2,240	7,880	5,017,600	17,651,200
19x5	1,981	6,762	3,924,361	13,395,522
19x6	2,175	7,245	4,730,625	15,757,875
	11,705	40,459	23,199,011	79,921,827

available. Table 5.1 gives us the following figures for inclusion in the formulas:

$$\sum_{i=1}^{n} x_i = 11,705$$

$$\sum_{i=1}^{n} y_i = 40,459$$

$$\sum_{i=1}^{n} x_i^2 = 23,199,011$$

$$\sum_{i=1}^{n} x_i y_i = 79,921,827$$

$$n = 6.$$

Substituting these figures into the formula for b we get

$$b = \frac{6(79,921,827) - (11,705)(40,459)}{6(23,199,011) - (11,705)^2}$$

$$b = 2.72$$

correct to two decimal places. Substituting this value for b and certain of the other values calculated above into the formula for a gives

$$a = \frac{40{,}459 - 2.72(11{,}705)}{6}$$

$$a = 1{,}436.90.$$

With these two calculated values of a and b we may now write our straight line equation

$$y' = 1{,}436.90 + 2.72x.$$

It is estimated that semi-variable costs comprise a fixed element of £1,436.90 per annum and a (linear) variable element of £2.72 per unit of output. By adding these figures to the other variable and fixed costs of Jacobin Ltd we estimate the total cost (TC) of the firm in the coming year as

$$TC = (5{,}850.00 + 1{,}436.90) + (6.40 + 2.72)x$$
$$TC = 7{,}286.90 + 9.12x.$$

5.3 The Coefficient of Correlation

We have now derived an expression that may be used to predict the future level of semi-variable (and hence total) costs. As yet, we do not have any indication as to how accurate the predictions are likely to be. Figures 5.2 and 5.3 show two sets of observations. The straight line determined by the least squares method of linear regression has the same equation in each case, but it seems likely that most people would put more reliance on its predictions in the case shown in Figure 5.2 than in the one shown in Figure 5.3. The statistic normally used for assessing the goodness of fit of a regression line is known as the coefficient of correlation.

It is again outside the scope of this text to consider the derivation of the formula normally used for calculating the coefficient of correlation but in its most workable form it may be written

$$r = \frac{n.\sum_{i=1}^{n} x_i y_i - \left(\sum_{i=1}^{n} x_i\right)\left(\sum_{i=1}^{n} y_i\right)}{\sqrt{n.\sum_{i=1}^{n} x_i^2 - \left(\sum_{i=1}^{n} x_i\right)^2} \sqrt{n.\sum_{i=1}^{n} y_i^2 - \left(\sum_{i=1}^{n} y_i\right)^2}}$$

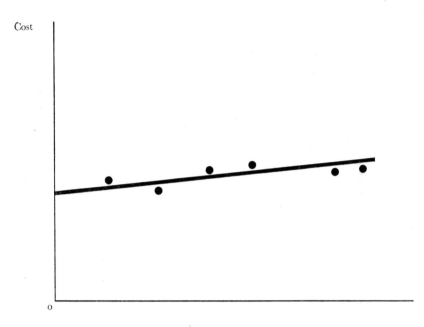

FIGURE 5.2

where r is the coefficient of correlation to be found and the other terms are as defined previously.[5] In the nature of the expression, r will take a value between -1 and $+1$. If the value is close to -1 or $+1$ the fit of the line is said to be good. For values near to 0 the fit is poor and the observed relationship between x and y is non-existent. A negative r indicates that x and y are negatively correlated; as x increases so y decreases. Graphically this relationship would be represented by a downward sloping curve. In our example the correlation is positive, y increases as x increases, and so we would expect the calculated coefficient of correlation to assume a value between 0 and $+1$. The higher the value of r, the better the fit of our calculated regression line to the observed data.

5. For a more detailed explanation of the derivation of this formula see
   FREUND, J E and WILLIAMS, F J, Modern Business Statistics, Sir Isaac
   Pitman and Sons Ltd, 1959, pages 307–310.

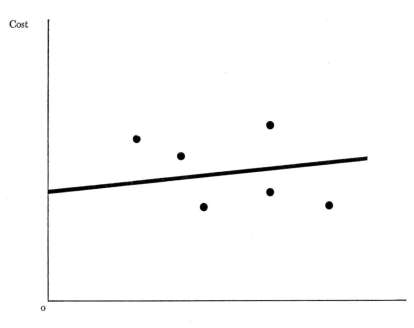

Cost

O

Output

FIGURE 5.3

The interpretation of r is not easy unless it assumes a value of 0, $+1$ or -1. If r is zero the fit of the line is so poor that it will be of no assistance in predicting values of y from observed or expected values of x. In the other two cases ($r = +1$ or $r = -1$) all observations used in the test fall on a straight line and the fit is perfect. For an interpretation of other values of r we turn to Freund and Williams: '... generally, if the coefficient of correlation for observations on two variables x and y is equal to r, then $100.r^2$ per cent of the variation of the y's may be accounted for by the relationship with the variable x'.[6] If r equals 0.80 in a particular test then 64% of the variations in the observed values of y are predicted (but not necessarily caused) by changes in the observed values of x. The statistic r^2, or $100.r^2$, is often used in practice to indicate the goodness of fit of a regression line.

6. FREUND, J E and WILLIAMS, F J, Modern Business Statistics, Sir Isaac Pitman and Sons Ltd, 1959, pages 315.

Reverting to our example of the semi-variable costs of Jacobin Ltd, we may calculate the value of r by substituting into the equation the relevant values from Table 5.1. The only expression in the equation for r for which we do not have a value in Table 5.1 is $\sum_{i=1}^{n} y_i^2$. The calculation of this figure is shown in Table 5.2.

Table 5.2

y_i	y_i^2
6,314	39,866,596
5,630	31,696,900
6,628	43,930,384
7,880	62,094,400
6,762	45,724,644
7,245	52,490,025
	275,802,949

Substituting into the equation for r gives us

$$r = \frac{6(79,921,827) - (11,705)(40,459)}{\sqrt{6(23,199,011) - (11,705)^2} \; \sqrt{6(275,802,949) - (40,459)^2}}$$

$$r = +0.95.$$

With a value for r of $+0.95$ we conclude that $100 \cdot r^2$, or just over 90%, of the variations in the observed values of y, the observed levels of semi-variable costs, are accounted for by changes in x, the observed output levels. This gives an indication of the level of confidence we should have in our calculated regression line. In this case the level of confidence will be high as the large majority of changes in semi-variable costs are explained by changes in output. The high value of r^2 also gives some indication that the assumption of linear cost behaviour was a good one.

5.4   Advantages and Limitations of Cost Prediction by Linear Regression
The advantages of this sort of statistical approach to cost estimation are similar to those claimed for a formal model building approach in

other areas of decision making: greater consistency, less subjectivity,
more insight into the functional relationships facing the firm and so on.
The calculations look lengthy but most calculating machines are
capable of handling them quickly and efficiently. There are, however,
a number of limitations to the approach:

(i)   In Chapter 4 we discussed the relevant range within which
        certain approximations of cost behaviour might be acceptable
        (page 56). The same concept may be applied to the equation
        derived by linear regression. It may describe cost behaviour
        within the range of the observations used to determine it but
        may not apply to levels of output outside that range. This
        explains the paradox sometimes encountered in cost-output
        exercises when the regression line has a formula of the order
        $- a + bx$. It seems to follow that at a zero output level total cost
        is negative. But a zero output level would be outside the range
        of observations used to determine the equation of the line, and
        consequently cannot be costed from the equation with
        confidence.

(ii)   A quite large number of observations are necessary to impart
        validity to the calculated equation for cost prediction. It may
        be necessary to go back a number of years to obtain a sufficient
        number of observations. A problem may arise where, for
        example, circumstances have changed in such a way that
        available historical data are no longer reliable indicators of
        future trends. The problem may be reduced by using cost
        figures for periods of less than one year, provided that the data
        are available in such shorter periods and that there are no
        seasonal patterns to distort the picture.

(iii)   In interpreting the statistic r we noted that it provides an
        indication of the variations in the values of y that may be
        accounted for by changes in the value of x. This does not
        necessarily imply a causal relationship between y and x. For
        example, it may be that a third variable affects the values of
        both y and x and consequently any rise in y is not caused by,
        although it will be accompanied by, a rise in x. Freund and
        Williams cite the well known example of the high positive

correlation between the level of teachers' salaries and the amounts spent on the consumption of alcohol.[7] This may not be a causal relationship, but a case of two factors being influenced by a common variable: the general standard of living.

(iv)   In addition to the points mentioned above there are some technical problems that may complicate the application of linear regression. Most of them bear imposing names, such as heteroscedasticity, multicollinearity, serial correlation and autocorrelation. A detailed consideration of their nature is outside the scope of this text.[8]

The example of Jacobin Ltd was designed to give an indication of the usefulness of linear regression in cost prediction. Other statistical techniques are available for dealing with more complex situations than that postulated. The computational capacity of electronic computers may lead to these techniques more frequently finding their way into practical usage. The example given was primarily intended to illustrate the principle of applying the work of statisticians to decision making problems.

7. FREUND, J E and WILLIAMS, F J, Modern Business Statistics, Sir Isaac Pitman and Sons Ltd, 1959, page 316.
8. For brief descriptions see YEOMANS, K A, Applied Statistics, Penguin, 1968, pages 103–105 and page 208 (for heteroscedasticity), page 331 (for multicollinearity) and page 208 (for serial correlation and autocorrelation).

6 Cost-Volume-Profit Analysis

6.1 Cost–Volume–Profit Relationships

At the beginning of Chapter 4 we suggested that to achieve its objective (assumed to be the maximisation of current cash resources) a firm should consider the combined effect on both its cost and revenue functions of changes in the level of output. We now turn to the consideration of these relationships. This area is normally known as cost–volume–profit analysis or, a term perhaps more familiar to accountants, break-even analysis. The problem is to estimate what output levels the firm should choose for its products.

To simplify the analysis and, it is hoped, to illustrate better the basic principles involved we shall make three initial assumptions. First, we shall assume that the firm is producing only one product. The implications of dropping this assumption are considered later in this chapter. Second, it will be assumed that none of the resources used by the firm is in short supply. The problem of scarce resources is discussed further in Chapters 7 and 8. Finally, we shall continue with the assumption that stock levels will not change, and consequently that the entire output produced during a period is expected to be sold during that period.

We shall consider first the economist's approach to optimal output level decisions and then compare this with the accountant's concept of break-even analysis. We shall also consider the role of the principles developed in previous chapters in solving this sort of problem.

6.2   *The Economist's Approach*

Given an assumed objective of profit maximisation the economist defines the output level a firm should adopt as being determined by

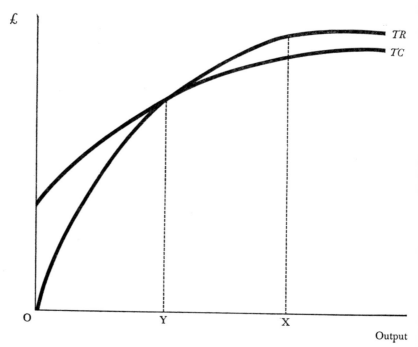

FIGURE 6.1

two sets of relationships; the cost–volume relationships facing the firm and the demand (price–volume) relationship for the (single) product. Suppose a firm expects total cost (*TC*) and total revenue (*TR*) functions as shown in Figure 6.1. At output level OX the difference between total revenue and total cost is at its greatest—that is, profit is maximised.

The point of maximum profit may be determined algebraically using elementary differential calculus.[1] Profit (or cash surplus) may be described by the equation

$$P = TR - TC$$

where P is profit and TR and TC total revenue and total cost respectively. To find the output level (x) at which profit is maximised we differentiate P with respect to x and set the answer equal to zero:

$$\frac{dP}{dx} = \frac{dTR}{dx} - \frac{dTC}{dx} = 0$$

The optimal output level occurs where

$$\frac{dTR}{dx} = \frac{dTC}{dx},$$

provided that

$$\frac{d^2P}{dx^2} < 0.[2]$$

dTR/dx is the firm's marginal revenue and dTC/dx its marginal cost. The former reflects the amount of additional revenue that will accrue to the firm from a marginal increase in production, the latter the incremental cost to the firm of such an increase. In effect, the decision rule is that production should be increased so long as incremental benefits are greater than incremental costs. This condition is satisfied until the two become equal (marginal revenue equals marginal cost). Beyond this point increases in production will give rise to extra costs greater than the incremental benefits, resulting in a fall in total profits, assuming that marginal revenue does not increase again relative to marginal cost.

1. A good introductory text for those not familiar with differential calculus is FERRAR, W L, Calculus for Beginners, Clarendon Press, 1967. A simpler, but sometimes lengthier, method of solution is suggested on page 90.
2. This is the second order condition which establishes that the slope of the profit curve is about to become negative—that is, that we have reached a point of maximum rather than minimum profit.

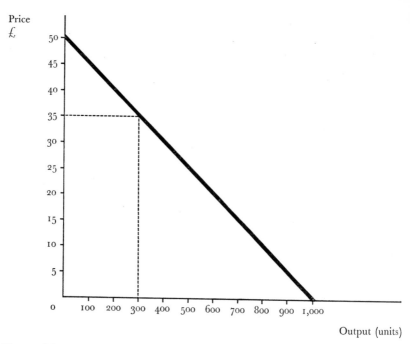

FIGURE 6.2

Let us consider an example to illustrate this approach. Suppose a firm has a total cost function described by the expression

$$TC = 4{,}000 + 15x$$

which might have been derived using the methods discussed in Chapter 5. The firm manufactures only one product. x is the amount of that product expected to be produced and sold in the coming year. The firm expects that the higher the price charged, the lower the quantity of the product it will be able to sell during the year (the normal economic assumption). More precisely, the expected relationship is shown by the demand curve in Figure 6.2.[3] For example, if the firm sets a price of £35 per unit it expects to be able to sell 300 units. It

3. It will be difficult to estimate the expected relationship in practice. In order to develop the cost–volume–profit framework we shall assume, at this stage, that the relationship is known.

can be seen from Figure 6.2 that for each increase in output of 100 units the price the firm will be able to charge, if it is to sell all of its output, falls by £5. For each increase in output of one unit the attainable price falls by £$\frac{5}{100}$ or 5p. Thus we may establish the equation of the price line as

$$SP = 50 - 0.05x$$

where SP is the selling price in pounds and x the output in units.

The total revenue (TR) accruing to the firm will be the product of the price per unit and the number of units to be produced (and sold):

$$TR = SP.x = 50x - 0.05x^2.$$

As we now have expressions describing the total cost and total revenue functions of the firm we are able to construct Figure 6.3 which shows graphically the relationship between the two functions.

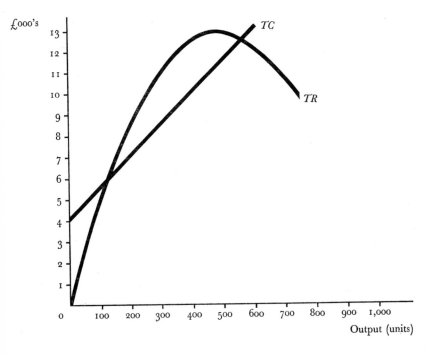

FIGURE 6.3

Reverting to our previous consideration of the economist's approach we note that dTR/dx measures the *slope* of TR and dTC/dx the *slope* of TC. So long as TR is steeper than TC it is worthwhile increasing production, for total revenue is increasing at a faster rate than total cost. By finding that value of x which equates dTR/dx and dTC/dx we determine the output level at which the slope of TR is no longer steeper than TC. Above this level TC is steeper than TR and further production is unprofitable.

Using the total revenue and total cost functions for the firm we may derive marginal revenue and marginal cost expressions as follows:

$$TR = 50x - 0.05x^2$$

$$\text{Marginal revenue} = \frac{dTR}{dx} = 50 - 0.1x \tag{1}$$

$$TC = 4{,}000 + 15x$$

$$\text{Marginal cost} = \frac{dTC}{dx} = 15.$$

The optimal output level is that value of x which equates these two expressions:

$$50 - 0.1x = 15$$
$$x = 350.$$

An alternative approach, for those not familiar with the differential calculus, is to estimate the optimal output level by trial and error. In Table 6.1 we give details of the profits or losses expected at output levels between 100 and 800 units, in intervals of 100 units. The figures suggest that the optimal level lies between 300 and 400 units. Further trial and error calculations will pinpoint the optimal figure of 350 units. An advantage of this approach is that it provides the firm with an indication of the sensitivity of expected profit to changes in the level of output.

The highest price at which the firm will be able to sell the optimal output is found by substituting for x in the selling price expression:

$$SP = 50 - 0.05x$$
$$= 50 - 0.05(350)$$
$$SP = £32.5.$$

Table 6.1

Output x	Total revenue – $(50x - 0.05x^2)$ £	Total cost = $(4,000 + 15x)$ £	Profit/(loss) $(35x - 0.05x^2 - 4,000)$ £
100	4,500	5,500	(1,000)
200	8,000	7,000	1,000
300	10,500	8,500	2,000
400	12,000	10,000	2,000
500	12,500	11,500	1,000
600	12,000	13,000	(1,000)
700	10,500	14,500	(4,000)
800	8,000	16,000	(8,000)

This will give total revenue of £11,375(£32.5 [350]) and total cost of £9,250 (£4,000 + £15 [350]), a profit of £2,125.

If the firm produces one extra unit it will incur additional costs of £15 and receive additional revenue of £14.9 (£50 − £0.1 [351]), from equation (1), a net deficit of £0.1. If it produces only 349 units it will avoid costs of £15 and lose revenue of £15.1 (£50 − £0.1 [349]), again a reduction in profit of £0.1. Any greater increases or decreases over 350 units will lead to greater reductions in profit. Provided we are able to estimate the firm's total revenue and total cost functions, and express them in a convenient mathematical form, the economist's analysis should lead to an optimal output level decision.

6.3   Break-even Analysis and Flexible Budgeting
The break-even chart used frequently by accountants is, in a sense, no more than a linear approximation of the sort of graph illustrated in Figures 6.1 and 6.2. To describe it as a break-even chart is misleading and in many cases may be an inadequate representation of the variety of functions it serves. The initial purpose of the break-even chart may have been primarily to indicate to the firm the level of output at which total revenue just covers associated total cost. Nowadays, in conjunction with the 'relevant range' concept introduced earlier (page 56), it may be intended to provide an estimate of profit

at different output levels as is the economist's analysis discussed in the previous section.

Suppose a firm, which manufactures a single product, is considering its production plan for the coming year. It estimates that the following figures are relevant to that plan, within the output range (the relevant range) 6,000 to 24,000 units:[4]

Selling price	£5.0 per unit
Fixed costs	£30,000
Semi-variable costs:	
Fixed element	£10,000
Variable element	£1.0 per unit
Variable costs	£2.0 per unit.

From this information we may construct, by geometrically summing the various cost categories, the break-even chart shown in Figure 6.4.

The break-even point, X, at which total revenue just covers total cost may be read from the diagram (20,000 units). Alternatively we might determine X algebraically by solving the following equation:

$$TR = TC$$
$$5.0X = 40,000 + 3.0X$$
$$X = 20,000.$$

A number of alternative algebraic solutions are possible. For example, we could divide the fixed element of total cost (£40,000) by the contribution to fixed costs made by each unit of the product manufactured and sold (£[5.0 — 3.0]). Again, we get a solution of 20,000 units.

This break-even output information may be useful to the firm in assessing the probability of making a profit in the coming year. (How likely is it that an output of at least 20,000 units will be produced and sold?) It will be less useful in guiding the firm to an optimal output decision. (What output level will produce the highest profit?) Within the limits imposed by the relevant range, it is apparent from the chart that the maximum output (24,000 units) will produce the highest profit. It also seems that, without the constraint imposed by the

4. The cost classifications used correspond to those discussed in Chapter 4.

relevant range, any increase in output above 24,000 will apparently increase profit. In theory, the optimal level is infinity. This conclusion follows from the assumed linearity of the cost and revenue functions and is one of the weaknesses of the method.

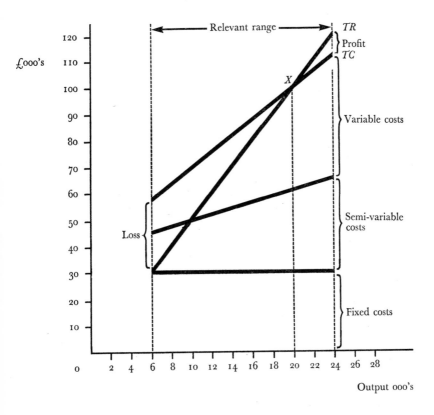

FIGURE 6.4

In practice, the firm will probably incur its fixed costs in large indivisible lumps and the total 'fixed cost' function will be analogous in form to the step variable functions discussed in Chapter 4. Suppose that the firm we are considering has a total cost function whose variable element remains £3.0 per unit. But now assume that the 'fixed' element of total costs increases in lumps at various output levels as follows:

Output range	Total fixed cost
	£
0– 5,000	10,000
5,001–10,000	15,000
10,001–15,000	20,000
15,001–20,000	25,000
20,001–25,000	35,000
Above 25,000	Increases by £15,000 for each additional 5,000 units.

It is not worthwhile producing above 25,000 units, for each additional 5,000 units above that level yield a contribution to fixed costs of £10,000 (£[5.0–3.0] × 5,000), less than the increase in fixed costs of £15,000.

The break-even chart reflecting the revised cost figures is shown in Figure 6.5. It is apparent from this chart that maximum profit is attained at output levels of either 20,000 or 25,000 units, where

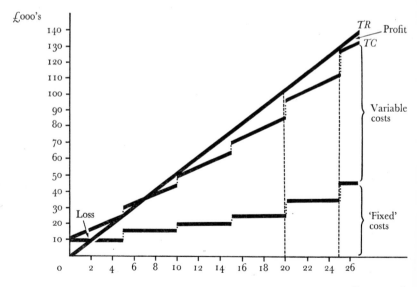

FIGURE 6.5

the difference between total revenue and total cost is £15,000. As the total cost function is not a smooth curve there is no simple algebraic formula that will yield either the break-even points or the level of output that maximises profit. The break-even point (or points) is normally determined most easily from a graph. The output level (or levels) leading to maximum profit may also be observed from the chart. Alternatively,

Table 6.2

| | \multicolumn{5}{c}{*Output level (units)*} | | | |
	5,000	10,000	15,000	20,000	25,000
	£	£	£	£	£
Variable costs (£3.0 per unit)	15,000	30,000	45,000	60,000	75,000
Step fixed costs	10,000	15,000	20,000	25,000	35,000
Total costs	25,000	45,000	65,000	85,000	110,000
Sales revenue (£5.0 per unit)	25,000	50,000	75,000	100,000	125,000
Profit	—	5,000	10,000	15,000	15,000

we may calculate the profit at various feasible levels of output, choosing the one that yields the highest profit. This is the basis of a procedure known as *flexible budgeting*.

Where step costs are involved, the optimal output level will often lie at one of the points just before a new injection of fixed costs becomes necessary. We may therefore decide that we shall obtain a satisfactory approximation to the optimal plan if we prepare flexible budgets for output levels of 5,000, 10,000, 15,000, 20,000 and 25,000 units. The calculations are shown in Table 6.2 and confirm the results obtained by examining the break-even chart. The optimal output levels are 20,000 and 25,000 units. To reinforce the earlier claim that an increase in output above 25,000 units is not worthwhile consider the profit at,

say, 30,000 units; it is £10,000.[5] This is less than the profit expected at
20,000 or 25,000 units and consequently an inferior output level in
terms of the firm's assumed objective of maximising cash resources.

Both the break-even chart and flexible budgets lead us to the
same answer. Which is superior? The flexible budgeting approach
boasts a numerical precision that graphical analysis may not always be
able to match. On the other hand, a break-even chart illustrates
graphically the relationship between cost and profit for all output
levels. It may be a simpler means of conveying the often complicated
nature of this relationship to those responsible for taking decisions. In
addition, the break-even chart shows the range of output levels at
which profits are expected to be made. In our example the firm expects
to make a profit at all output levels between 7,500 and 25,000 units.
Had we extended the graph to cover higher volumes we should have
seen that output levels between 25,000 and 30,000 units and between
32,500 and 35,000 units were also expected to be profitable. This
indication of the profitable ranges might prove useful to the firm in
assessing the sensitivity of profit to deviations from the planned level of
output.

Both break-even charts and flexible budgets have their
advantages. It seems probable that a combination of the two techniques
will lead to better decisions being made than if either method is used
in isolation. Graphical analysis could be used to establish the general
ranges within which production is at its most profitable and flexible
budgeting could be applied to 'sharpen up' the figures.

In the form discussed above, break-even analysis suffers some
limitations. We have already mentioned that revenues and costs are
normally assumed to be linear in a break-even chart. The implications
of this assumption are discussed in Chapter 7 (pages 117–118). In

5.

	£
Variable costs	90,000
Step fixed costs	50,000
Total costs	140,000
Sales revenue	150,000
Profit	10,000

addition, it is normally assumed that total cost changes only as a result of changes in the level of output. For the purpose of exposition, we have assumed so far that this is the case in our analysis of cost–volume–profit relationships. If other factors influence total cost and revenue behaviour then break-even analysis, like the other methods considered, must be adapted accordingly. Multi-product firms create further difficulties, which are mentioned in the next section.

6.4   Multi-product Firms

Before leaving our initial consideration of cost–volume–profit relationships we shall examine briefly the effects of relaxing one of the simplifying assumptions made at the beginning of this chapter, namely, that the firm produces only one product. Are the techniques of break-even analysis and flexible budgeting as useful and simple to apply to multi-product firms as to those manufacturing a single product? Provided that none of the firm's input factors is in short supply there seems to be no reason why the techniques should not be equally useful and straightforward. All that is required is a separate break-even or flexible budgeting analysis of each product.

Two particular problems may arise if this approach is followed. First, there may be interdependences between the production or demand functions of two or more of the firm's products, i.e., the demand for, or cost of manufacturing, a product may be affected by the demand for or level of production of some other product (see Chapter 7, pages 119–120 for examples). If this is the case it will be necessary to consider the interdependent products together. This should present no particular problems if the output mix of the products is determined outside the analysis by the nature of the interdependence. The combination of interdependent products may be dealt with as though it were a single product. If the product mix is not determined outside the analysis it will be difficult to deal satisfactorily with different products on one graph.

Second is the difficulty of the fixed costs of the firm. Should these be allocated on some basis between the various products for inclusion in the individual break-even charts and flexible budgets? Following the principles developed earlier for dealing with fixed costs, the answer will depend on their nature. If the costs clearly relate to a particular product and would not be incurred if that product were not manufactured then they should be regarded as fixed costs of the product and included in the analysis relating to it. If, on the other hand, the costs are in the nature of general overheads, created by the existence of the firm itself rather than of any particular product, then to allocate them to individual products will be misleading, for the reasons discussed in Chapters 3 and 4, and may lead to incorrect output decisions. Initial output decisions should be made for each product, regardless of general fixed costs. Then a budget should be prepared for the firm as a whole, based on the optimal output levels for each product and incorporating the general fixed costs of the firm, to ensure that the predicted contributions from the individual products are sufficient to cover the non-allocable fixed costs. The construction of a break-even chart for the firm as a whole seems unnecessary in these circumstances and may be confusing as it depends on a prior management decision on optimal output mix which management may not be able to make rationally without a cost–volume–profit analysis.

If one or more of the firm's resources is scarce there will be an effective limit on the total output of the firm. How should the constrained resources be allocated between the various products? The answer depends on how effectively each product uses the scarce resources. This problem we proceed to discuss in the next chapter.

7 Decision Making with Scarce Resources: Linear Programming

7.1 Internal Opportunity Cost

In Chapter 3 we considered the relevant cost of a particular course of action where none of the resources used by a firm is scarce. This part of the total cost of a decision alternative we called the external opportunity cost. We developed the appraisal criterion that production or investment opportunities should be expanded or accepted so long as the extra revenue they produce is greater than their external opportunity cost.

We shall now consider the situation where, because of a restriction on the availability of one or more of its resources, a firm is unable to accept every opportunity whose revenue exceeds its external opportunity cost. This is defined as a situation of scarce resources. (A particular resource is said to be scarce if the firm has insufficient supplies of it to accept all opportunities expected to produce positive contributions.) It may be necessary to impute additional costs to the use of these resources, over and above their external opportunity costs, to ration their use. These additional costs we shall call internal opportunity costs.[1] We shall consider first the situation where only one of the firm's resources is scarce and then extend the analysis to situations of two or more scarce resources.

7.2 The Situation with One Scarce Resource

The internal opportunity cost of using a scarce resource on a particular opportunity depends on the best alternative use to which that resource could have been put had the particular opportunity not been undertaken. To determine this figure we need to know not only the 'profitability' of accepted opportunities but also the potential 'profitability' of rejected ones. We need a means of choosing between a range of opportunities where acceptance of all of them is precluded by the existence of a scarce resource. The method utilised in the following example is an adaptation of the familiar accounting concept of maximising profit per unit of the limiting factor used. It involves ranking opportunities so as to prefer those that yield the highest contribution per unit of the scarce resource that they require.[2]

Let us examine the case of Jago Ltd which is considering its production plan for the coming year. It has reduced the range of products worth considering as manufacturing possibilities to the five shown in Table 7.1. The selling price of each product, if manufactured, will be as shown in the table. The company's estimate of the maximum amount it will be able to sell at that price is also given. The external opportunity cost of manufacturing each product comprises raw materials, manufacturing labour, machine user cost and variable overheads. Details of the cost of these resources, together with the

1. Some writers prefer to define the internal opportunity cost of a resource to include its external opportunity cost. Thus the internal opportunity cost represents the full cost of using that resource. The terminology used in this text implies that the total cost of using a resource is the sum of its external and internal opportunity costs. Unfortunately there seems to be no generally accepted terminology and either is satisfactory provided that it is used consistently.
2. This approach is also discussed in CARSBERG, B V, Introduction to Mathematical Programming for Accountants, George Allen and Unwin, 1969, pages 40–1 and HORNGREN, C T, Cost Accounting—a Managerial Emphasis, 2nd Edition, Prentice-Hall, 1967, pages 413–14.

number of units of raw materials, manufacturing labour hours and machine hours required to manufacture one unit of each product, are given in Table 7.1. There is unlikely to be any restriction on the availability of the resources included as variable overheads, or on the availability of any other resources apart from those specified below, for any likely production plan.

The problem facing Jago Ltd is to derive a production plan that will maximise the company's cash resources at the end of the coming year. We shall assume that no products will be manufactured that cannot be sold during the year at the prices included in Table 7.1, and that at present the company has no stock of any of the products.

The optimal plan will be that combination of the available products that yields the maximum total contribution to fixed costs and profit. If none of the resources to be used is expected to be scarce during the coming year then Jago Ltd will satisfy its objective best by producing all of the products up to the limits imposed by the anticipated demand constraints, as each product yields a positive contribution to fixed costs and profit.

Suppose however that the company expects to have available only 6,000 machine hours during the coming year and that this limit is not to be exceeded. All other input factors required are expected to be available in any likely quantity at the external opportunity costs shown in Table 7.1. To produce all five of the products up to the expected demand limits would require 8,880 machine hours, 2,880 more than the number available.[3] To enable us to choose between the products, we need a means of ranking them that will ensure that all products accepted for manufacture make a more efficient use of the scarce resource, in terms of the company's objective, than any that are

3.	Product	Maximum demand	Machine hours per unit	Total machine hours
	L	400	3	1,200
	M	440	5	2,200
	N	900	2	1,800
	O	570	4	2,280
	P	350	4	1,400
				8,880

Table 7.1

Product:	L	M	N	O	P
Selling price:	£11.0	£15.0	£15.0	£10.0	£25.0
External opportunity cost:	£0.5	£0.5	£1.5	£1.0	£2.0
Raw materials					
Manufacturing labour	3.0	1.5	4.5	3.0	7.5
Machine user cost	1.5	2.5	1.0	2.0	2.0
Variable overheads	3.0	2.5	2.0	2.0	3.5
	—	—	—	—	—
	8.0	7.0	9.0	8.0	15.0
Contribution per unit:	3.0	8.0	6.0	2.0	10.0
	═══	═══	═══	═══	═══
Maximum expected demand (units)	400	440	900	570	350
Raw materials required (units)	4	4	12	8	16
Labour hours required	4	2	6	4	10
Machine hours required	3	5	2	4	4

Table 7.2

Product	Contribution per unit (£)	Machine hours per unit	Contribution per machine hour (£)	Ranking
L	3.0	3	1.0	4
M	8.0	5	1.6	3
N	6.0	2	3.0	1
O	2.0	4	0.5	5
P	10.0	4	2.5	2

rejected. The simplest suitable means of ranking involves expressing
the contribution of each product in terms of the scarce resource
(in this case machine hours). The products are ranked according to
the contribution they produce per unit of the scarce resource
they require.

The ranking calculation is shown in Table 7.2. Product N
makes the most efficient use of scarce machine hours and the company
should produce as many units of N as are possible within the demand
constraint, i.e. 900 units. The next best product is P and this should
also be produced up to its demand limit of 350 units. The procedure
continues until the available machine hours are exhausted. It may be
seen from Table 7.3, which shows the optimal plan, that products
M, N and P are produced up to their demand limits while the amount

Table 7.3

Product	Ranking	Amount produced	Machine hours required	Contribution (£)
N	1	900	1,800	5,400
P	2	350	1,400	3,500
M	3	440	2,200	3,520
L	4	200	600	600
O	5	—	—	—
			6,000	13,020

of product L that can be produced is constrained by the availability of machine hours. After producing M, N and P up to their respective demand limits 600 machine hours remain unused (6,000 − [1,800 + 1,400 + 2,200]). As each unit of L requires 3 machine hours, 200 units of L may be produced.

The plan yields a total contribution to fixed costs and profit of £13,020. This can be demonstrated to be the best attainable by considering the effect of utilising one of the machine hours presently being applied to producing L (the least desirable of the acceptable products) and transferring it to the production of O, the only (and consequently the best) product not included as part of the optimal plan. Total contribution will fall by £1.0 (lost on L) and increase by £0.5 (gained on O) a net decrease of £0.5. The substitution is not worthwhile. Similarly, it is not worthwhile substituting O for any of the accepted products. The plan is the best available from the five products under consideration.

Similarly, it will not be profitable to substitute for L any new product that subsequently becomes available unless it produces a contribution for each machine hour it uses of at least £1.0. Within the framework of the optimal production plan £1.0 represents the marginal return from one machine hour. It is the internal opportunity cost of one (marginal) machine hour. We should accept a new opportunity, as a substitute for product L, only if the difference between its incremental revenue and its total opportunity cost is positive.[4] The total opportunity cost, where only one resource is scarce, may be defined as the sum of external opportunity cost and internal opportunity cost, the latter representing the contribution from the best alternative use of the scarce resource.

Had we been given the internal opportunity cost of one machine hour in addition to the external opportunity costs of other factors we could have determined which products were worthwhile without having ranked them. We would have chosen those whose selling prices

4. We could equally well appraise the worthwhileness of a new opportunity by calculating the contribution it produces per unit of the scarce resource it uses and ranking it with existing opportunities. Where more than one scarce resource is involved, however, this method is computationally complicated.

Table 7.4

Product:	L	M	N	O	P
Selling price (Table 7.1):	£11.0	£15.0	£15.0	£10.0	£25.0
External opportunity cost (Table 7.1):	£8.0	£7.0	£9.0	£8.0	£15.0
Internal opportunity cost (machine hours required × £1.0)	3.0	5.0	2.0	4.0	4.0
Total opportunity cost:	11.0	12.0	11.0	12.0	19.0
Surplus/(Deficit)	0.0	3.0	4.0	(2.0)	6.0

exceeded their total opportunity costs. The calculations are shown in
Table 7.4. Products M, N and P show a surplus and should be pro-
produced up to their respective demand limits. Product L shows
neither surplus nor deficit and should be produced only in so far as
machine hours are available after producing M, N and P. Product O
shows a deficit and should not be produced.

Unfortunately, before we can determine the internal opportunity
cost of the scarce resource we need to know the optimal plan,
otherwise we do not know which is the 'marginal' product, on which
the internal opportunity cost is based. Nevertheless, once the initial
plan is established, the internal opportunity cost may be useful in
assessing marginal changes without having to re-solve the complete
problem.

7.3 The Situation with More than One Scarce Resource

Suppose that Jago Ltd, in addition to the machine hours constraint
of 6,000, expects to have available only 17,500 units of raw material
during the coming year. How might it now determine its optimal plan
and the internal opportunity costs of the two scarce resources? Will the
approach used in the previous section, based on one of the two scarce
resources, produce an optimal result?

Let us consider the plan that will emerge if the products are
again ranked according to the contributions per machine hour. Now
we have to consider not only the total machine hours but also the total
raw materials required, the latter being restricted to 17,500 units. The
new plan is shown in Table 7.5. Raw materials are fully used but
1,425 machine hours remain available. Raw materials represent an
effective constraint on production and the amount of product M that
can be manufactured is determined by the raw materials available after
products N and P have been produced to their demand limits. 1,100
units of material are available for production of M (17,500 − [10,800
+ 5,600]) and as each unit of M requires 4 units of raw material,
275 units may be produced.

To check the plan in Table 7.5 for optimality we again consider
whether any change in the plan is possible that will increase the total
contribution. Consider the effect of switching one unit of raw material
from production of N to production of L. This will cause a fall in the

Table 7.5

Product	Contribution per unit (£)	Machine hours per unit	Raw materials per unit	Amount produced	Machine hours required	Raw materials required	Contribution (£)
N	6.0	2	12	900	1,800	10,800	5,400
P	10.0	4	16	350	1,400	5,600	3,500
M	8.0	5	4	275	1,375	1,100	2,200
L	3.0	3	4	—	—	—	—
O	2.0	4	8	—	—	—	—
					4,575	17,500	11,100
Amount available					6,000	17,500	
Amount unused					1,425	—	

production of N of $\frac{1}{12}$ of a unit and an increase in the production of L of $\frac{1}{4}$ of a unit.[5] The substitution is feasible for it requires no extra raw materials and the extra machine hours it requires are available. It is also profitable because total contribution rises by £0.75 ($\frac{1}{4} \times$ £3.0), gained on L, and falls by £0.5 ($\frac{1}{12} \times$ £6.0), lost on N, a net increase of £0.25. Thus the original plan is not the best available.

Similar problems would arise if we were to rank the products according to contribution per unit of raw materials required. The difficulty is that products are ranked differently depending on whether machine hours or raw materials are chosen as the limiting factor. If the rankings were identical under each criterion there would be no contention. As it is we need a technique that takes into account the products' relative use of the two scarce resources. A popular tool available for solving this sort of problem is linear programming.

7.4   Linear Programming: Formulation
Linear programming is the most simple of the mathematical programming techniques available as aids to the decision maker. It is widely used in fields other than production planning but it is this function, as an aid to the solution of business decision problems, that is of particular interest to us here.

The general form of the linear program in this sort of situation is as follows:

$$\text{Maximise } C = \sum_{i=1}^{n} c_i\, x_i \tag{1}$$

$$\text{Subject to } \sum_{i=1}^{n} a_i\, x_i \quad \leq \quad A$$

$$\vdots \qquad\qquad \vdots \quad \vdots \tag{2}$$

$$\sum_{i=1}^{n} f_i\, x_i \quad \leq \quad F$$

$$x_i \quad \leq \quad D_i \tag{3}$$

$$x_i \quad \geq \quad 0 \tag{4}$$

5. It may not be possible to make fractional adjustments to the production plan but the principle seems valid; if it is worthwhile switching one unit of raw material from N to L it will probably be worthwhile transferring more than one unit, thus enabling whole units of L to be manufactured.

(1) is known as the objective function, which is normally an equation (model) describing total profit or, more precisely, contribution. We wish to maximise the value of this expression (C). x_i is the amount of product i to be produced and sold during the coming period. The program is designed to find the optimal value of each x_i. c_i is the contribution that one unit of product i makes to fixed costs and profit.

The other expressions are inequalities that define the constraints to be observed in maximising the objective function. The constraints under (2) represent restrictions on the availability of input factors (resources). For example if A is the total amount of input factor A expected to be available during the planning period and a_i is the amount of that input factor required to produce one unit of product i, then the constraint $\sum_{i=1}^{n} a_i x_i \leq A$ requires that the total amount of factor A used (the left-hand side of the inequality) does not exceed the amount available. Similarly the available amounts of the other scarce input factors, B . . . . . F, must not be exceeded.

In inequality (3), a special case of the general constraints under (2), D_i represents the maximum demand expected for product i during the coming period. Assuming no production for stock, the firm will not want to produce more of product i than it is able to sell.

The constraints included under (4) are known as non-negativity constraints. They are technical requirements to ensure that negative production quantities for any of the products are not included in the optimal plan. This may seem an obvious and hence unnecessary stipulation. However, many linear programming problems are solved on computers which would admit negative numbers on the same terms as positive numbers unless told not to do so. Computer logic would 'reason' that if it is better to produce a zero amount than a positive amount of a particular product then it will be better still to produce a negative quantity.

In all of the expressions in the general formulation, n is the number of products available for consideration as part of the production plan. Other refinements are possible within the general formulation than those specifically mentioned here; provided the expression may be stated in a linear form there is usually no reason why it should not be incorporated. The description 'linear programming' merely reflects that the equations and inequalities included are linear (i.e., they may be represented by straight lines).

Linear programming, then, is suitable for solving problems where the objective is to maximise (or minimise) the value of some linear function subject to constraints (expressed as linear inequalities) which must not be violated.

To illustrate the general formulation of linear programming problems we shall return to the example of Jago Ltd, and continue to assume that machine hours and units of raw materials are limited, in the coming year, to 6,000 and 17,500 respectively. The other data necessary for the formulation are shown in Table 7.1. If we let x_1 equal the quantity of product L to be produced and sold during the coming year, x_2 the quantity of product M to be produced and sold during the coming year, and so on, then we can formulate the linear programming problem as follows:

$$\text{Max } C = 3x_1 + 8x_2 + 6x_3 + 2x_4 + 10x_5$$
$$\text{s.t. } 3x_1 + 5x_2 + 2x_3 + 4x_4 + 4x_5 \leq 6{,}000$$
$$4x_1 + 4x_2 + 12x_3 + 8x_4 + 16x_5 \leq 17{,}500$$
$$x_1 \leq 400$$
$$x_2 \leq 440$$
$$x_3 \leq 900$$
$$x_4 \leq 570$$
$$x_5 \leq 350$$
$$x_i \geq 0 \text{ (where } x_i = x_1 \ldots \ldots x_5).$$

The solution to this problem will provide us with those values of x_1, x_2, x_3, x_4 and x_5 that maximise the value of the objective function, i.e. total contribution, and hence with an optimal plan. The values will be such that none of the constraints is violated.

7.5   Linear Programming: Solution

There are a number of techniques available for the solution of linear programming problems. All but the simplest problems are normally solved on a computer and it is not proposed to discuss the methods used in detail here.[6] Simple linear programming problems, e.g. where only two products are to be considered, may be solved with the aid of a graph. As this method of solution also serves to illustrate a number of the principles involved in more complicated methods of solution we shall apply it to a worked example.

Helios Ltd manufactures two products, the Widget and the Didget. Each Widget which is sold produces a contribution of £5 and each Didget £4. All input factors required to manufacture the two products are freely available at their market prices with the exception of labour time, storage space and a special component GBD 4. In the coming year Helios Ltd expects to have available a maximum of 30,000 labour hours, 10,000 square feet of storage space and 33,000 units of GBD 4.

Each Widget requires 15 labour hours, an average of 2 square feet of storage space per annum and 11 units of GBD 4. Each Didget requires 6 labour hours, an average of 4 square feet of storage space per annum and 12 units of GBD 4. No restriction is expected on the demands for the two products. Helios Ltd is seeking a production plan for the coming year that will maximise total contribution to fixed costs and profit from the two products. There is to be no production for stock.

If we let x_1 equal the number of Widgets to be produced and sold in the coming year and x_2 the number of Didgets similarly to be produced and sold then we may formulate the problem as a linear program:

$$\text{Max } C = 5x_1 + 4x_2 \qquad \text{(objective function)}$$
$$\text{s.t.} \quad 15x_1 + 6x_2 \leq 30{,}000 \qquad \text{(labour constraint)}$$
$$2x_1 + 4x_2 \leq 10{,}000 \qquad \text{(storage space constraint)}$$
$$11x_1 + 12x_2 \leq 33{,}000 \qquad \text{(GBD 4 constraint)}$$
$$x_1, x_2 \geq 0 \qquad \text{(non-negativity constraints)}$$

6. Those interested in a further examination of the methods available for solving more complex problems might refer to BAUMOL, W J, Economic Theory and Operations Analysis, 2nd Edition, Prentice-Hall, 1965, Chapter 5, for the simplex method or CARSBERG, B V, Introduction to Mathematical Programming for Accountants, George Allen and Unwin, 1969, Chapters 4 and 5 for an alternative description of the method, based on repeated substitution.

The first step in the graphical solution is to plot the various constraints. In Figure 7.1 we start by drawing axes representing possible production levels of Widgets and Didgets, x_1 and x_2. Any point

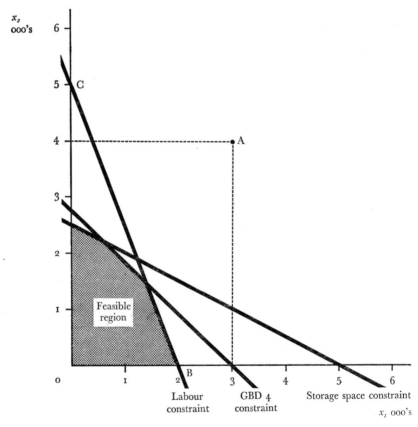

FIGURE 7.1

on the graph represents a production plan. For example point A represents a production of 3,000 Widgets (x_1) and 4,000 Didgets (x_2). Our first task is to define a region, known as the *feasible region*, which covers all points, or solutions, that yield production plans not violating any of the constraints.

Consider first the two non-negativity constraints. $x_1 \geq 0$ implies that the solution must lie on or to the right of the x_2-axis.

Similarly $x_2 \geq 0$ implies that the solution must lie on or above the
x_1-axis.

The boundary lines describing the other three constraints will
all be linear as the constraints themselves are expressed as linear
inequalities. If an input is fully utilised up to the limit imposed by the
available amount of the resource then the inequality describing the
constraint will become an equality. For example, if labour is fully
utilised then the values of x_1 and x_2 will be such as to satisfy the
equation

$$15x_1 + 6x_2 = 30,000.$$

There is an infinite combination of values of x_1 and x_2 which
satisfy this equation. To construct the line which connects them all, we
need only calculate two of the combinations as we know the line is
straight. The two we shall calculate are shown as points B and C in
Figure 7.1. Point B represents a value of zero for x_2 and consequently
a value of 30,000/15 or 2,000 for x_1. Point C represents a value of zero
for x_1 and hence a value of 5,000 (30,000/6) for x_2. By connecting these
two points we construct a line representing the boundary imposed by
the labour constraint; the solution must lie to the left of and below
this line. By a similar process we may construct constraint lines for
storage space and for the special component GBD 4. The lines are
shown in Figure 7.1.

To be acceptable a solution must not violate any of the five
constraints. All such solutions lie within the shaded area, designated
the feasible region, on the graph in Figure 7.1. They are known as
feasible solutions. Any production plan represented by a point outside
the feasible region will violate at least one of the constraints and will
not be acceptable.

The next step is to find the solution, from within the feasible
region, that is *optimal*, giving the highest value to the objective function.
To do this we shall make use of what are normally known as iso-profit
lines. An iso-profit line connects all points on the graph that represent
production combinations yielding the same profit. As our assumed
objective is to maximise total contribution to fixed costs and profit our
lines will connect all points representing production combinations
producing the same total contribution, i.e. giving a constant value to

the objective function. For example, the broken line DE on the graph in Figure 7.2 links all solutions that yield a total contribution of £20,000.

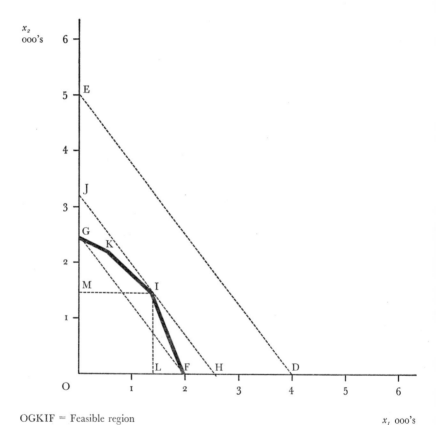

OGKIF = Feasible region x_1 ooo's

FIGURE 7.2

    The construction of the line is similar to the method used to construct the constraint boundary lines; as the line is straight we need only calculate two points lying on it to be able to draw the whole line. For simplicity we choose the two points representing a zero production of one product and a balancing figure for the production of the other. For the £20,000 constant contribution line, if x_2 equals zero then x_1 must equal 4,000 (£20,000/£5) and if x_1 equals zero, x_2 must equal

5,000 (£20,000/£4). Similarly, we might construct an iso-profit line for a contribution of £10,000. This is the broken line FG in Figure 7.2.

There are an infinite number of constant contribution lines, all having a negative slope equal to the ratio of the contribution from a Widget to the contribution from a Didget ($\frac{5}{4}$). The objective is to discover the product combination represented on the highest contribution line, i.e. the one which will yield the highest total contribution.

From the graph it is apparent that line HJ is the highest profit line attainable that includes a product mix not outside the feasible region (OGKIF). The line HJ is tangential to the feasible region at point I. It is a general rule of linear programming solutions that the optimum will lie somewhere on the boundary of the feasible region; to any point within the feasible region, there corresponds another on the boundary having a greater contribution. Unless the iso-profit lines have the same slope as one of the constraint boundary lines there will always be an unique optimal solution at the intersection of two constraint lines, as at the intersection of the labour and GBD 4 constraint lines in our example.

The solution represented by point I is optimal. It is within the feasible region and yields a higher contribution than any other point in the feasible region. We might ascertain the production plan it represents by reading from the graph the values of x_1 and x_2 (OL and OM respectively). However this method may lack precision and as an alternative we might utilise our new-found knowledge that the optimal plan involves using labour and the special component GBD 4 to their available limits. In other words, the inequalities describing these two constraints in the initial linear programming formulation become equalities at the optimal point, i.e.

$$15x_1 + 6x_2 = 30,000$$
$$11x_1 + 12x_2 = 33,000.$$

Solving these as simultaneous equations we obtain values, correct to one decimal place, for x_1 of 1,421 and for x_2 of 1,447.5. The optimal plan is to produce 1,421 Widgets and 1,447.5 Didgets.[7]

7. It is assumed, at this stage, that it is possible to produce and sell fractional units of the products.

Let us check that this plan will not lead to the violation of any constraints. The usage of the scarce resources implied by the plan is shown in Table 7.6. With the exception of the small rounding error affecting the special component GBD 4, none of the constraints is violated. This confirms the feasibility of the plan.

Table 7.6

Usage of scarce resources

Labour:	$15(1{,}421) + 6(1{,}447.5) = 30{,}000$	
Storage space:	$2(1{,}421) + 4(1{,}447.5) = 8{,}632$	
GBD 4:	$11(1{,}421) + 12(1{,}447.5) = 33{,}001$[8]	

The total contribution expected from the plan may be determined by substituting the optimal values of x_1 and x_2 into the objective function:

Total contribution $= £5(1{,}421) + £4(1{,}447.5) = £12{,}895.$

The optimality of this contribution could be confirmed by checking that there is no feasible substitution that would lead to a higher total contribution. Subject to the limitations of the method, discussed in the next section, the solution obtained by linear programming should be optimal.

Using the graphical framework, we might have calculated the optimal solution differently. As we know that the optimum solution (or solutions if the iso-profit lines are parallel to a boundary of the feasible region) will lie at one of the corner points of the feasible region we might simply have calculated the contribution at each of these points and chosen the one with the highest contribution, thus avoiding the need for iso-profit lines. Alternatively, we could have dispensed with the graph altogether and calculated the values of x_1 and x_2 at the corner points by solving simultaneously all possible pairs of constraint equations, including the non-negativity constraints. After discarding solutions that violated other constraints, the solutions remaining would

8. This small error is the result of rounding to one decimal place in an earlier calculation.

have represented the production plans at all corner points of the feasible region. From amongst them, we could have chosen the combination of x_1 and x_2 that yielded the highest contribution.[9]

7.6 Limitations and Assumptions of Linear Programming

There are a number of limitations to the linear programming approach, some of which stem from the assumptions implicit in the technique. The usefulness of linear programming models for decision making depends on how well they simulate the conditions under which the firm actually operates.

As we have seen, linear programming models assume linear relationships between the variables. This has a number of practical implications. For example, one implicit assumption is that whatever the quantity of a particular product offered for sale, up to the level of any demand constraint which is included in the model, the selling price remains constant. The usual economic assumption is that the greater the number offered for sale, the lower will be the average price obtainable in the market (except in perfect markets, which are rarely found in practice). If a firm feels that it will be able to sell up to X units at a price of £Y it may include a constraint to this effect in its linear programming model. However the optimal solution may suggest an output less than X units and it may be that the firm could sell this lower output at a price in excess of £Y. If the price is increased accordingly, the original plan may no longer be optimal. In this situation, the first formulation may be revised in the light of the first solution and the procedure repeated until a satisfactory position is reached.

A further implication of the linearity assumption is that each unit of output of a particular product requires a constant amount of each input factor, i.e. each successive unit of an input factor used on a particular product produces the same output quantity of that product. In the case of labour, for example, it is assumed that the work force is equally efficient in all situations, ignoring the possibility that labour needs time to 'warm-up' at the start of a production run or that men

---

9. In effect, this is the technique employed in the simplex method of solution, referred to in footnote 6 of this chapter.

and women become more weary and less efficient towards the end of the
run, and so on.

Further, the model depends on our being able to divide the
total cost function of the firm into fixed and variable elements. Where
step cost functions exist (see pages 59–60) they must be treated with care.
Some may be reasonably approximated by a linear function while
others may, within defined ranges, be regarded as fixed. Where neither
of these treatments seems appropriate some improvisation may be
necessary. For example the program may be run at different maximum
output levels, corresponding to the points at which steps in total costs
occur; step costs would be ignored in the formulation but adjusted
manually in comparing contributions at each output level.

It is implied also that however many units of an input factor are
bought, up to any constraint that may be assumed, the same price will
be paid for each unit. This may fail to take account of discounts for
bulk buying, increased prices as the available supply diminishes, and
so on. Where these implied assumptions are not representative, or
reasonably representative, of the actual conditions facing the firm,
the use of a linear programming model may be inappropriate.

The linear programming solution may not be optimal if the
input cost and price data used do not represent the external
opportunity costs of the particular factors. For example, to maximise
product contributions calculated on an historical cost basis may lead
to a solution that is inconsistent with the maximisation of current cash
resources.

As with the models discussed previously we have ignored the
time factor, i.e. we have assumed that no adjustments for interest
costs are needed. Nor have we dealt explicitly with the problem of
uncertainty. In practice, linear programming is a most useful aid to
tackling the uncertainty problem. Once the initial program is
formulated, say on the basis of 'best estimates', the values of individual
elements may be altered and the program re-run rapidly to determine
the effect of the change on total contribution. This sensitivity analysis
enables the firm to form an opinion as to the sensitivity of total
contribution to exogenous changes or estimating errors in the values of
individual input factors. Because much of the decision making cost is
in the initial formulation of the problem, rather than in its solution

(which will probably be on a computer) the incremental cost of the sensitivity analysis may be relatively low.

There are a number of other factors that the linear programming model for Helios Ltd does not take into account. The solution involved producing 1,447.5 Didgets. It may be that the assumption that fractional units of products could be produced and sold is invalid. If so, the optimal solution will have to be in terms of integer output levels. Where fairly large output levels are involved, as in the case of Helios Ltd, this may be achieved by rounding down any fractional output levels to the nearest whole number. So the production plan for Helios Ltd would be 1,421 Widgets and 1,447 Didgets. Where small output levels are envisaged and each output unit is large relative to the total, such a process of rounding may not lead to a solution that is a good approximation to the optimum and a more refined form of programming may be required. This is known as integer programming and involves the inclusion of extra constraints to prohibit solutions involving fractional output levels.[10]

A further factor that was ignored in handling the problem of Helios Ltd was the possibility of interdependence between the demands for Widgets and Didgets. Demand for the products, on the one hand, may be complementary. An example would be a firm manufacturing propelling pencils and the leads that are used in them. A fall in the number of pencils sold may lead to a fall in the number of leads demanded. Alternatively, the products may be substitutes for each other when a fall in the number of one product sold will be associated with a rise in the demand for others. An example would be an organisation manufacturing more than one sort of breakfast cereal. The implicit assumption of linear programming is that the demand functions for the various products under consideration are independent of each other. Where this is not a valid assumption a more refined mathematical programming approach is required.

An analogous problem may arise where there are inter-dependences between the input factors required to manufacture two

---

10. A detailed study of integer programming is outside the scope of this text. A good introduction is contained in BAUMOL, W J, Economic Theory and Operations Analysis, 2nd Edition, Prentice-Hall, 1965, Chapter 8.

or more of the products. For example, a farmer cannot produce milk, meat and hides independently of each other. They all come from the same input factor, the cow, and the final amounts produced are interrelated. In situations like this, the basic programming model may require development by the addition of extra constraints. Often, however, if the implied assumptions discussed in this section do not hold, we must resort to one of the non-linear programming techniques that are available.[11]

We mention three further points that are not strictly limitations of linear (and other) programming techniques but rather warnings to exercise care in their use. Similar caveats apply to many other mathematical business problem solving techniques. The first concerns the existence of costs and benefits that are not readily quantifiable and hence may not be incorporated easily into the program. For example, the firm may lose customer goodwill if it fails to produce a full line of products. It may be possible to treat this as a demand interdependence problem if the necessary quantification can be achieved. On the cost side, there is the possibility of industrial action if the optimal plan involves laying off part of the labour force. The uncertainties involved make it difficult to predict the likelihood and potential cost of a strike, for example. It may be that the firm wishes to ensure that the plan selected does not involve reducing the number of men employed on production below a specified minimum. In the case of Helios Ltd, for example, a constraint is already included limiting the maximum number of labour hours. Suppose the firm also requires that a minimum of 18,000 hours be worked to reduce the probability of industrial action. This could be achieved by inserting a further constraint

$$15x_1 + 6x_2 \geq 18,000$$

which would ensure that at least 18,000 labour hours were required in the production plan.[12]

11. For an introduction to non-linear programming see BAUMOL, W J, Economic Theory and Operations Analysis, 2nd Edition, Prentice-Hall, 1965, Chapter 7.
12. If the requirement is merely that the labour should be employed for a minimum of 18,000 hours (not necessarily on productive work), the

The second point is that linear programming will only yield a solution that is optimal for the available input data. Any opportunities that are not included in the formulation cannot be considered. It is important for the decision maker to ensure that a satisfactory range of feasible opportunities is taken into account unless there is some obvious reason for excluding any of them.

The final point concerns the implied rigidity of the constraints. As we are using a precise mathematical technique to solve our problem the input data must also be precise. A limit of 30,000 labour hours is interpreted in the solving of the problem at its face value, and not, for example, as 30,000 plus or minus 10%. In practice, it is likely that the constraints will have some degree of flexibility, particulary if the possibility of paying increasing prices for further supplies is not rejected. Dual prices, to be discussed in the next chapter, provide useful information for assessing the worthwhileness of paying a larger incremental price for a greater quantity of an input factor.

At first sight, the limitations of linear programming seem imposing. Yet many of them stem from the implied assumption of linear cost functions, and a number of statistical studies have presented evidence suggesting that within fairly wide relevant ranges firms are confronted with cost functions that may be reasonably approximated by linear expressions.[13] In addition many firms are already using linear programming techniques on a wide variety of business problems, with apparently satisfactory results.[14] The evidence suggests that linear programming is one of the more useful tools developed during the past few years.

---

original constraint limiting the maximum number of labour hours becomes:

$$15x_1 + 6x_2 \leq L$$

and the following additional constraints are included:

$$L \leq 30,000$$
$$L \geq 18,000 \text{ (or } -L \leq -18,000)$$

13. See, for example, JOHNSTON, J, Statistical Cost Analysis, McGraw-Hill, 1960, particularly Chapters 4 and 5.

14. For examples of some applications see MOORE, P G and HODGES, S D (eds), Programming for Optimal Decisions, Penguin, 1970, Part Two.

8 Dual Prices

8.1 Internal Opportunity Cost with Two or More Scarce Resources

In the previous chapter we considered means of determining an optimal production plan where one or more of a firm's resources is scarce. We also demonstrated that in the case of a single scarce resource the internal opportunity cost of one unit of that resource is given by the extra return which could be secured if one extra unit were available. We now turn to the problem of determining internal opportunity costs of resources where more than one of them is scarce.

Within the linear programming framework, is there a way of determining the marginal contribution each scarce resource is making towards fixed costs and profit? There is, and the marginal return is normally known as the *dual price* or *shadow price* of the particular resource. Given the type of formulation used in the last chapter, the dual price of a resource measures by how much total contribution will fall if the available amount of that resource falls by one (small) unit. If the program is solved on a computer the dual price is normally readily available. Its calculation is part of the simplex method of solving linear programming problems. However, as in the previous chapter, we shall continue with the graphical method of solution to illustrate the principles involved in calculating dual prices, and the economic meaning which may be ascribed to them.

123

Example

Let us continue with the case of Helios Ltd, whose linear programming problem was formulated on page 111. We shall consider the effect on total contribution of reducing the availability of each of the three

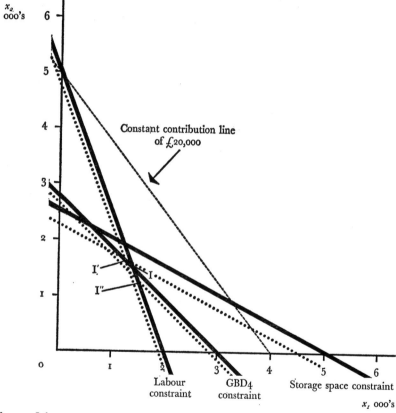

FIGURE 8.1

scarce input resources in turn. The total contribution from the original optimal plan was £12,895 (page 116). In the first instance we shall consider the effect of reducing the availability of each resource by 1,000 units to avoid the infinitesimal figures that would result from a reduction of only one unit. To find the reduction that would be caused by a reduction of a single unit we may, in this case, divide the calculated loss in total contribution by one thousand. This method would not be valid if such a substantial reduction in resource availability were to lead to a change in the marginal product combination or in those resources representing an effective constraint on production (in the case of Helios Ltd labour hours and units of special component GBD 4) but the principles illustrated may be applied to smaller changes. The original constraint lines are shown on the graph in Figure 8.1. The dotted lines represent the boundaries that would be operative if the available amount of each resource were to be reduced by 1,000 units.

Labour hours: Suppose that Helios Ltd expects to have available only 29,000 labour hours in the coming year. The expected availability of the other two scarce resources is unchanged. The boundary line of the feasible region represented by the labour constraint will move downwards and to the left. It is apparent from the graph in Figure 8.1 that the new optimal production plan is represented by point I', where the revised labour constraint line and the original GBD 4 constraint intersect. To determine the production plan represented by this point we solve the following simultaneous equations:

$$15x_1 + 6x_2 = 29,000$$
$$11x_1 + 12x_2 = 33,000.$$

This gives values, correct to one decimal place, of 1,315.8 for x_1 and 1,543.8 for x_2. The production plan is summarised in Table 8.1, which also shows that the new plan produces a total contribution £141 less than the original. Correspondingly, a reduction of one hour in the amount of labour time available would lead to a fall in the value of the optimal plan of £0.141.

Storage space: It can be seen from Figure 8.1 that a reduction in the available storage space of 1,000 square feet, the other two constraints remaining at their original levels, would not affect the optimality of the original plan. The optimal point would be I on the graph in Figure 8.1 and the total contribution £12,895. It follows that a reduction of one square foot in the available storage space would also lead to no fall in the value of the optimal plan.

Table 8.1

	Quantity	Contribution per unit £	Total contribution £
Revised production plan			
Widgets	1,315.8	5	6,579
Didgets	1,543.8	4	6,175
Revised total contribution			12,754
Original total contribution			12,895
Decrease due to a reduction of 1,000 in available labour hours			141
Decrease caused by a reduction of one in available labour hours		$£\dfrac{141}{1,000} = £0.141$	

Special component GBD 4: A reduction of 1,000 units in the number of GBD 4 components available, amounts of labour time and storage space originally available remaining unchanged, would lead to an optimal plan represented by point I″, as may be seen from Figure 8.1. The boundary line of the feasible region described by the GBD 4 constraint moves downwards and to the left. The new optimum lies where the revised GBD 4 constraint intersects the original labour hours constraint. The relevant values of x_1 and x_2 are determined by solving the following simultaneous equations:

$$15x_1 + 6x_2 = 30,000$$
$$11x_1 + 12x_2 = 32,000.$$

This gives values, correct to one decimal place, of 1,473.7 for x_1 and 1,315.8 for x_2, implying the production plan shown in Table 8.2. This plan yields a contribution £263 less than the original one. Correspondingly, a fall of one unit in the availability of GBD 4 would lead to a decrease of £0.263 in total contribution.

The reductions in total contribution caused by falls of one unit in the available supplies of the three scarce resources are summarised

Table 8.2

Revised production plan	Quantity	Contribution per unit £	Total contribution £
Widgets	1,473.7	5	7,369
Didgets	1,315.8	4	5,263
Revised total contribution			12,632
Original total contribution			12,895
Decrease due to a reduction of 1,000 in available units of GBD 4			263
Decrease caused by a reduction of one in available units of GBD 4		$£\dfrac{263}{1,000} = £0.263$	

in Table 8.3. The figures measure the marginal return a single unit of
each resource is yielding within the framework of the optimal plan.
As was mentioned earlier, they are called the dual, or shadow, prices
of the resources. Their use as measures of the internal opportunity cost
of using the resources is discussed in the next section.

8.2   Interpretation of Dual Prices

It is worthwhile to note first the equivalence of the dual price of a
scarce resource discussed above and the marginal return of a scarce
resource, when it is the only scarce resource, discussed in Chapter 7.

Table 8.3

Resource	Fall in total contribution if amount available decreases by one unit (Dual Price) £
Labour time	0.141
Storage space	0.000
Special component GBD 4	0.263

The latter is no more than a special case of a dual price and could equally well have been determined by solving the single scarce resource problem as a linear program. Both measure the amount by which total contribution would fall if the firm were deprived of one unit of the scarce resource. Provided the scarce resource remains an effective constraint on production, both also measure the amount by which total contribution would rise if an additional unit of the resource were available.

Table 8.4

Extra sales revenue ($\frac{1}{3}$ unit of L):		£3.67
Extra external opportunity costs ($\frac{1}{3}$ unit of L):		
Raw materials	£0.17	
Manufacturing labour	1.00	
Variable overheads	1.00	
	——	2.17
Increase in cash flow (excluding machine cost):		1.50

What, then, is the total opportunity cost of using one marginal unit of a scarce resource? Let us revert to the example of Jago Ltd introduced in Chapter 7. When only machine time was scarce we determined that the marginal return, the dual price, of one machine hour within the optimal plan was £1.0 (page 104). How much should Jago be willing to pay to obtain one extra machine hour? If the extra hour were available it would be used best in increasing production of product L, the marginal product. The information in Table 7.1 (page 102) indicates that an extra $\frac{1}{3}$ unit of L could be produced, as each unit of L requires 3 machine hours. Using the figures in Table 7.1 we may draw up the statement in Table 8.4 which shows the cash flow effects of this change. At the moment, we shall ignore the cost of machine time, for our problem is to determine the maximum amount Jago Ltd will be willing to pay for the extra machine hour. The statement shows that one extra machine hour would lead to an increase in net cash flow of £1.50.

A similar calculation would show that a decrease in the cash flow of £1.50 would result from a reduction of one hour in the available machine time. Jago Ltd should be willing to pay up to £1.50 to acquire an extra machine hour or to avoid losing one of those already available. This amount is the sum of the external opportunity cost, £0.5, and the internal opportunity cost (the dual price), £1.0, of one machine hour. In a situation of scarce resources the total opportunity cost of using a marginal unit of a resource is the sum of its external and internal opportunity costs, the latter being given by its dual price.

Two further observations on dual prices may be of interest. We have seen that costs that are fixed regardless of the decision to be taken have no external opportunity cost. However, if these costs represent a resource that is scarce there may be a relevant cost attached to the resource: the total opportunity cost of using one unit will equal its dual price.

In the problem of Helios Ltd, the dual price of storage space was zero (Table 8.3). The same is true of any resource that does not represent an effective constraint on production, even if the available supply of the resource is expected to be limited.[1] Neither a marginal increase nor a marginal decrease in the available amount of the resource will lead to any change in the optimal plan. The cost of using such a resource is its external opportunity cost which reflects the only sacrifice involved in utilising it.

8.3 Limitations of Dual Prices

As dual prices are the products of a linear programming framework they suffer the same limitations and are based on the same assumptions as are relevant to linear programming (see pages 117–121). Within these limits, they are useful indicators of the internal opportunity cost of using scarce resources.

However, there is a further reason for caution when dual prices are being used. They measure contribution changes resulting from marginal increases or decreases in resource availability. A large

1. Strictly, the supply of all of a firm's resources will be limited in an absolute sense for there will be a limit on the amount of the resource available in the world. For practical purposes, however, a resource need only be regarded as scarce if its supply is limited within the range of any production plan a firm is likely to adopt.

increase in the availability of a particular resource may mean that it is no longer an effective constraint on production and its dual price becomes zero. Consider the case of Helios Ltd, if it finds a supplier who is willing to provide up to an extra 11,000 units of the special component GBD 4. The company has to decide how much, over and above the market price previously charged, it would be willing to pay for extra units. It might be argued that as the dual price of a resource measures the maximum amount a firm would be willing to pay, over and above the external opportunity cost, to obtain one further unit of that resource, then Helios Ltd should be willing to pay up to 26.3p (the dual price) for each of the extra 11,000 units of GBD 4.

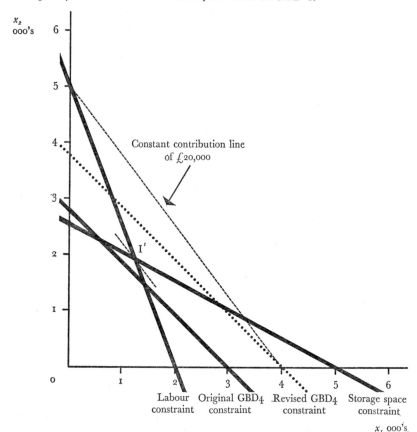

FIGURE 8.2

If we re-calculate the optimal plan, reflecting the increased availability of GBD 4 but ignoring, at present, the surcharge that will be paid on all units used over 33,000, then the increase in total contribution will measure the maximum amount, over and above the present market price, that Helios Ltd should be willing to pay for however many extra units of the special component are required. The revised GBD 4 constraint boundary is shown as a dotted line in

Table 8.5

Product	Quantity	Contribution per unit £	Total contribution £
Widgets	1,250	5	6,250
Didgets	1,875	4	7,500
Revised total contribution			13,750
Original total contribution			12,895
Increase in total contribution			855

Figure 8.2, and it is clear from the graph that GBD 4 is no longer an effective constraint. The optimal point is now I′, where the labour time and storage space constraints intersect. The relevant values of x_1 and x_2 are found by solving the following simultaneous equations:

$$15x_1 + 6x_2 = 30,000$$
$$2x_1 + 4x_2 = 10,000.$$

This gives values of 1,250 for x_1 and 1,875 for x_2, implying the revised production plan shown in Table 8.5.

The extra contribution under the new plan is £855, and the plan requires an extra 3,250 units of GBD 4.[2] The extra 3,250 units

2. Each Widget requires 11 units of GBD 4 and each Didget 12 units. Under the new production plan shown in Table 8.5 a total of 36,250 units of GBD 4 are required (11[1,250] + 12[1,875]). The previous plan required the maximum then available of 33,000 units and hence an additional 3,250 units are needed.

required increase total contribution by £855, an average of £0.263 per unit. The extra contribution obtainable from each unit of GBD 4 up to the amount required under the new plan remains equal to the dual price of 26.3p. But any units obtainable above this level do not increase total contribution at all as GBD 4 is no longer an effective constraint. Consequently it assumes a dual price of zero.

Dual prices alone are of little help in tackling problems like this where the change in resource availability is non-marginal The example suggests that we need to re-solve the problem incorporating the revised constraint(s) and compare the new optimal solution with the original plan.

8.4 Applications of Dual Prices

Provided the limitations mentioned in the previous section are borne in mind dual prices, discriminately applied, have a number of possible uses. First they provide an indication of which constraints are the most severe. In the original example of Helios Ltd, whose dual prices are given in Table 8.3 (page 127), it does not seem worthwhile devoting any time to endeavouring to find new storage space. The zero dual price attached to this resource indicates that it is not an effective constraint on production. The company might usefully seek ways of relieving each of the other constraints, for a relaxation of either of them will lead to an increase in total contribution. It may be misleading to argue that as the special component GBD 4 has a higher dual price than labour time it is, in some sense, more worthwhile to relieve it. The units chosen for measuring the constraint will affect the size of the dual price. For example, had we chosen labour weeks of 35 hours each instead of labour hours as the measure of labour time, the dual price would have been 35 times higher, i.e. £4.935, considerably greater than the GBD 4 dual price. The dual price per unit of the resource will be a good indicator of where effort should be directed to relieve constraints only if the expected cost per unit of relaxation is the same for each resource constraint.

A second application of dual prices may arise when new opportunities, not in the original plan, are presented for consideration. Dual prices reflect the best marginal use of resources within the framework of the optimal plan and, to be acceptable, a new opportunity should use the resources at least as profitably as this marginal use; in a situation of scarce resources the new opportunity, if accepted, will displace one or more of the opportunities included in the optimal plan. The new opportunity is a worthwhile substitute if it yields a surplus when the resources it requires are valued at total opportunity cost, including the dual price values of any scarce resources needed.

However, dual prices alone will not reveal precisely how the production levels of opportunities within the optimal plan should be adjusted: to determine this the firm must adopt some approximate method or re-formulate and re-solve the linear program. The dual prices act merely as a screening device for new opportunities, a useful function as it avoids the firm having to re-run the linear program for every new opportunity that emerges.

A third use arises when all decisions are not taken by a central decision making body with access to the linear program. Decentralised decision making may be in evidence particularly in divisionalised firms where each division enjoys a certain amount of decision taking autonomy. To reduce the chance that resources are used suboptimally, they should be charged to those responsible for decisions at their total opportunity cost. As this includes the dual price value of scarce resources, only projects at least as efficient at those included in the optimal plan should be accepted.

Applications of dual prices in the area of pricing, which are not unrelated to the second and third uses mentioned above, are considered in the next chapter.

9 Pricing Problems

In previous chapters we have discussed how a firm, with information giving predicted cost and revenue functions, might set about establishing a plan for its future operations which is optimal in terms of an assumed objective of maximising cash resources. We have considered the various forms cost functions might take and some ways in which firms might estimate their likely future shapes and magnitude. In this chapter we shall consider another important element in the setting of the plan: the price that the firm should charge for the products it is offering for sale.

Many factors influence the prices a firm may charge for its products and the maximum quantities it is able to sell at those prices. Advertising and other means of promotion, variations in quality, preferences of consumers and the behaviour of competitiors may all be assumed to play a part. A detailed consideration of how they do so is beyond the scope of this text.[1] We shall look at the basic pricing model of the economist and then consider the cost-plus method of pricing. We shall then discuss means of determining minimum prices

1. For an introduction to some of these considerations see BAUMOL, W J, Economic Theory and Operations Analysis, 2nd Edition, Prentice-Hall, 1965, pages 210–30.

and optimal prices where sufficient information is available about the demand conditions facing the firm.

9.1 *The Economist's Basic Pricing Model*

The economist's basic pricing model depends on the assumption that the firm is able to estimate its demand curve; i.e., the quantities of its product it will be able to sell at differing prices. Firms manufacturing more than one product present no particular problem, provided that there are no interdependences between the demand or production functions of the products and that output is not limited by the scarcity of resources. A separate analysis may then be undertaken for each product. The problem where these simplifying conditions do not hold is discussed later in this chapter.

The essence of the economist's approach was covered in Chapter 6 (pages 86–91), where output level decisions were discussed. The pricing decision is an integral part of the volume decision. The optimal output is determined by applying a marginal analysis to the cost and revenue functions of the product. The corresponding selling price is ascertained by substituting the volume figure in the model of the price–volume relationship or by reading the price from the demand curve graph. A simple example should illustrate this approach.

Suppose that a firm manufactures a single product and wishes to set its selling price for the coming year. The demand curve (selling price–volume relationship) for the product is estimated in the graph in Figure 9.1. The equation of the demand curve may be determined in this case by observation, as it is a straight line. For each extra 10,000 units which are offered for sale the average selling price of all units falls by £1.50. Thus an increase of one unit is expected to result in a reduction in selling price of £0.00015 (i.e. £1.50/10,000). As output approaches zero the selling price approaches £9. The equation of the demand curve is

$$SP = 9 - 0.00015x$$

where SP is the selling price and x the output.

If the price–output relationship is of the linear form of the demand curve in Figure 9.1, then its equation will be of the general form:

$$SP = a - bx$$

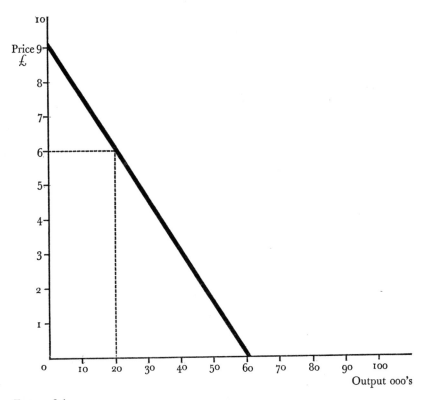

FIGURE 9.1

where SP is the selling price, x the output and a and b constants. In the above example a equals £9 and b equals £0.00015. From the general selling price equation we can derive a general equation describing marginal revenue (MR)[2]:

$$MR = a - 2bx. \qquad (1)$$

2. Total revenue (TR) is the product of selling price per unit (SP) and the number of units produced and sold (x), hence

$$TR = SP \cdot x = ax - bx^2.$$

Marginal revenue (MR) is determined by differentiating this expression with respect to x:

$$MR = \frac{\mathrm{d}TR}{\mathrm{d}x} = a - 2bx.$$

Let us further suppose that during the coming year the firm expects to incur fixed costs of £40,000 and a variable cost of £3 per unit produced and sold. The optimal selling price may be determined when the optimal output level is known. To calculate the optimal output level we follow the procedure described in Chapter 6 (page 87). This requires us to calculate the marginal revenue and marginal cost of the product and then to find the output level (x) that equates them. Marginal revenue (MR) is found by substituting the values in the example for a and b into expression (1) above:

$$MR = 9 - 0.0003x.$$

Marginal cost (MC) is found by differentiating the total cost function with respect to x, giving[3]

$$MC = 3.$$

The value of x that equates MR and MC is the optimal output level:

$$9 - 0.0003x = 3$$
$$x = 20,000.$$

We may calculate the optimal selling price by substituting this value of x into the selling price equation:

$$SP = 9 - 0.00015(20,000)$$
$$SP = £6.$$

Alternatively, we could have read this selling price from the graph in Figure 9.1.

This simple example illustrates one important but at times forgotten point about price setting, that the optimal price depends on both the cost and demand relationships facing the firm.

3. Total cost (TC) is
$$TC = 40,000 + 3x.$$

Differentiating this with respect to x gives us marginal cost (MC):

$$MC = \frac{\mathrm{d}TC}{\mathrm{d}x} = 3.$$

9.2   The Cost–plus Formula for Pricing

One of the most common myths surrounding pricing decisions seems to be that a substantial number of firms set prices solely by the use of a formula, based entirely on cost. Empirical work has been undertaken to test this supposition but little evidence has been produced to substantiate the view that prices are, in practice, set with no reference to demand conditions. A number of the researchers discovered procedures that took a cost–plus calculation as the first step in price determination but later included a consideration, often informal, of market demand conditions. In the light of these conditions the price initially calculated using the cost–plus formula was amended.[4]

In practice, the most difficult part of the pricing decision normally is to quantify expected future demand conditions. The cost–plus pricing formula avoids doing this as it contains no reference to demand forces. It is based entirely on cost. Because of this, and because the formula does seem to play some part, albeit a preliminary one, in the pricing policy of a number of firms, we shall investigate it further to see whether it might have some useful role to play in setting prices.

An example of the sort of form a cost–plus calculation might take is given in Table 9.1. The formula might be applied to a single job or to a whole product line. The direct costs of the job or product are calculated and to these is added an amount to recover production overheads (sometimes including depreciation), which may include both variable and fixed costs. A mark-up is also added, to cover selling and administrative overheads and profit, often designed to reflect what the decision maker regards as a 'reasonable' level of profit.

The use of such a formula is appealing. It looks objective and accurate and is relatively easy to apply. Furthermore, it enables

4. A sample of empirical evidence may be found in HALL, R L and HITCH, C J, 'Price Theory and Business Behaviour', *Oxford Economic Papers*, No. 2, May, 1939, reprinted in WILSON, T and ANDREWS, P W S (eds), Oxford Studies in the Price Mechanism, Clarendon Press, 1951; EDWARDS, R S, 'The Pricing of Manufactured Products', *Economica*, Vol. 19, August, 1952; PEARCE, I F, 'A Study in Price Policy', *Economica*, Vol. 23, May, 1956; and SKINNER, R C, 'The Determination of Selling Prices', *The Journal of Industrial Economics*, Vol. 18, July, 1970.

Table 9.1

Direct cost:		
Labour	—	
Materials	—	
Machine depreciation	—	—
Production overheads:		
x% on direct cost[5]		—
Total cost		—
Profit mark-up:		
y% on total cost		—
Price		—

management to delegate pricing decisions to subordinates. But the formula suffers from a number of defects and to apply it without affording them proper consideration may lead to sub-optimal pricing decisions.

First, the inclusion of direct costs in the formula may be criticised. Frequently, they are interpreted as costs that are easily traceable to a specific job or product. They may not accord with external opportunity cost.[6]

The problems of allocating, or recovering, fixed costs as a percentage of some item of direct cost, or on any other basis, were discussed in Chapter 4. If the overhead costs in the formula are fixed they will have to be paid whether or not the job being priced is undertaken. They are not avoidable costs but allocation may lead to their being treated as if they were. A firm may quote a cost–plus price that results in the contract going elsewhere even though it would have been justified in quoting a lower price, sufficient to cover total opportunity cost, and it would thereby have won the contract. For long-term pricing decisions overhead costs may be relevant. In the long

5. The overhead allocation is normally a pre-determined percentage of one or, as in this example, all of the items included as direct costs. It may be based on money values or on some other unit measure, e.g., labour hours.
6. See footnote 4 on page 59.

run all costs are avoidable. It does not follow that the sort of crude
allocation method normally employed in the cost–plus formula is the
best way of taking account of such costs.

There are other reasons for doubting the wisdom of overhead
allocation. To allocate, it is necessary to choose both a basis for the
allocation and a percentage to be applied to the base. The basis would
represent some measure of the resources to be used. In practice, the
precise choice varies according to the nature of the firm's business;
the choice of a monetary base, often adopted, may not be a satisfactory
measure of capacity utilisation.

The percentage applied to the base is frequently calculated by
reference to historical data. Whether these are a good representation of
the present and future is a matter for investigation.

The practice of overhead recovery as a percentage of direct cost
may lead to the magnification of errors in estimating direct cost. For
example, in the case of the Ferranti contracts to manufacture
Bloodhound Missiles for the Government, price was fixed by a
cost–plus formula. Direct labour was over-estimated by £732,000. This
caused an error of just under £5 million in total cost estimation when
the overhead percentage of 564% was applied.[7]

Another weakness of the cost–plus formula is the lack of an
explicit allowance for internal opportunity cost. We have noted that
the total cost of using a particular resource is the sum of its external
and internal opportunity costs. Apparently the cost logic of neither of
these concepts is recognised by proponents of the cost–plus method. It
is consequently not easy to impart any precise significance to either the
direct cost or the total cost figures of the formula.

The profit mark-up seems to imply an attempt to ensure that
the firm runs at a 'reasonable profit'. It is unlikely that this will accord
with the objective assumed in this text of maximising the cash
resources of the firm. This latter goal is most likely to be achieved if all
projects showing an expected surplus of revenue over total opportunity
cost are accepted.

The final defect to be noted here reflects a direct contrast with
the economist's approach. The cost–plus formula pays no regard to

7. See FLOWER, J F, 'The Case of the Profitable Bloodhound', *Journal of
Accounting Research*, Vol. 4, No. 1, Spring, 1966.

demand conditions. The formula will produce the same answer
whether the firm is operating in a highly competitive market or in a
near monopolistic position.[8] A seller cannot set both price and sales
volume without reference to the demand function for the particular
product. The sales volume will normally depend on the price set.

In many cases the difficulty encountered in estimating a firm's
demand curve inhibits the use of a formula for setting prices. The
cost–plus solution to this problem is simple: ignore it. However, this
approach contravenes a basic principle of good decision making: it is
preferable to obtain an answer that is approximately right than one
that is precisely wrong. Most decision situations are beset with
difficulties and to ignore them will almost inevitably lead to
sub-optimal courses of action being pursued.

In the context of pricing decisions we should recognise that
difficulties exist in forecasting demand conditions. Management
experience and intuition may well make an important contribution to
the decision. However, that is no reason to ignore the other information
needed to set prices: the relevant cost of particular courses of action
and the associated rules for ascertaining the minimum price that should
be set if a product is to be offered for sale. From this information the
price setter will be able to define more precisely the constraints imposed
on his pricing policies.

9.3   *Minimum Price Setting*
The minimum price which a firm should be willing to accept for a
particular job or product will not normally be affected by external
demand conditions for that product. It will depend on the costs of
manufacturing the product or undertaking the job. We shall apply the
principles of cost evaluation developed earlier to the establishment of
a minimum price rule. First we shall summarise briefly the planning
procedures assumed to be operative within the firm.

We shall assume that the firm plans its future strategy in
discrete time periods. We shall further assume that each of these periods
covers one year. At the beginning of each planning period an

---

8. This will not be the case if the firm varies its profit mark-up to take
   account of diverse market conditions on different contracts.

operational plan is drawn up covering next year's activities. The prices the firm is proposing to charge for its products will be components of the annual plan. Decisions taken at the time the plan is formulated we shall call planning point decisions, decisions taken at any other time are interim decisions. The principles already discussed in this text may be applied to decisions taken at planning points. In this section we shall consider, in particular, the importance of interim decisions, which are necessary to take advantage of opportunities not considered when the previous plan was formulated.

First let us consider the minimum pricing policy of firms that have no scarce resources. If there are no mutually exclusive opportunities the cost to the firm of using any of its resources is given by the external opportunity cost of the resource. Whether the firm manufactures one or many products and whether the decision is taken at a planning point or as an interim decision, the *minimum* price to be charged is given by the sum of the external opportunity costs of the resources required. At any price higher than this the firm will receive a contribution to fixed costs and profit.[9] We emphasise that the minimum price is the price below which the firm should not manufacture and sell a product. It is a starting point only. We shall consider the setting of an optimal price in the next section.

The establishment of a minimum price is more difficult where a firm manufactures more than one product, or undertakes more than one activity, and has scarce resources. First consider the problem of interim pricing decisions.[10] We shall assume that the firm uses linear programming techniques to derive its optimal plan at each planning point. As a result a dual price is available for each of the effective scarce resources. For an interim pricing decision the minimum price must be such that, if the price is obtained, the profit predicted in the (already ascertained) optimal plan will remain unchanged. Any price above this level will lead to an improvement in the original plan.

---

9. This may not provide an answer to another, more long term, decision facing the firm: whether it is worthwhile to continue in business at all, as to do so involves incurring certain fixed costs.
10. For a more detailed exposition see ARNOLD, J A, 'On the Problem of Interim Pricing Decisions', *Accounting and Business Research*, No. 10, Spring, 1973.

How might we calculate the minimum (interim) price that a firm should charge for undertaking a new opportunity? In Chapter 8 we noted that the dual price of a resource measures the contribution a marginal unit of that resource is making to fixed costs and profit. To be acceptable, a new opportunity must use the scarce resources at least as efficiently as their marginal use in the existing optimal plan; as the supply of the resources is limited the new opportunity will, if accepted, displace certain of the opportunities included in the optimal plan. The new opportunity must yield a contribution (incremental revenue minus external opportunity cost) greater than or equal to the dual price value of the scarce resources it requires.

This line of reasoning suggests an interim price rule where a firm manufactures more than one product and is in a situation of scarce resources. The price of the new opportunity must be at least sufficient to cover the external opportunity costs and internal opportunity costs (dual prices) of the resources it requires. However, this rule will not reveal how production levels of existing opportunities should be adjusted to accommodate the new one. To determine this it will be necessary to re-formulate and re-solve the linear programming problem, unless the new opportunity is so small that its impact on the overall plan may be approximated without too great a loss of accuracy.

Even though the minimum price rule normally fails to provide a revised production plan without re-running the linear program it is of some value. Without it, strictly it would be necessary to re-run the linear program each time a new opportunity emerges in order to assess its impact on the original optimal plan. To avoid this expense the minimum price rule might be used as a screening device for new opportunities. If the minimum price is clearly not attainable there is no feasible price at which the new opportunity can find its way into the optimal plan and no need to incur the expense of re-solving the linear programming problem.

Now consider the case where the minimum price calculation is to be effected at a planning point. We shall continue to assume a multi-product firm with scarce resources. If the product for which the minimum price is required is the only one for which no price has yet been set a similar procedure to the one outlined above may be followed. The remaining opportunities, for which selling prices have been decided, may be incorporated in a linear program which will give dual prices for the scarce resources. Using these as measures of the internal opportunity costs of the resources required for the opportunity to be priced, the minimum price will again be the sum of the external and internal opportunity costs of such resources.

The situation where none of the opportunities have been priced poses a problem that is somewhat artificial and whose solution is of little use. The minimum price for any particular opportunity is the external opportunity cost of the resources it requires.[11] At any higher price the firm receives a contribution to fixed costs and profit. The information is of limited value because the firm will need to consider the profitability of all opportunities relative to their need for scarce resources. The minimum price formula enables the firm to discard products that cannot feasibly be sold at a price high enough to cover their external opportunity costs. It fails to provide the answer to the crucial problem of choosing between those that remain. To tackle this problem it is necessary to move to a consideration of the relationship between the minimum price and the optimal price.

9.4 Optimal Price Setting

The transition from minimum to optimal price setting requires one crucial ingredient: information about demand conditions. Some factors that influence the demand for a particular product were mentioned in the introduction to this chapter. Although a detailed study of their impact on the price–volume relationships facing the firm is outside the scope of this text we shall briefly consider how the price setter might go about gathering information to assist him in quantifying the firm's demand functions.

Customer response to price changes in a particular product or range of products may be estimated on the basis of experience gained from previous price changes. It may also be tested by means of a market research survey, although people may not respond to actual changes in the same way as they claim they will react when confronted with a hypothetical increase or decrease.

11. As yet there is no plan and consequently the internal opportunity costs are not known.

Information about the likely reactions of competitors to price
changes may be obtained from an examination of previous experience
or by industrial espionage. The impact of advertising might be assessed
by controlled experiments backed up by market research surveys. In all
these situations the price setter will need to rely heavily on his own
intuition and judgement and on the expertise of other members of the
firm.

Example

To illustrate the principles involved in optimal price setting we shall
consider an example of pricing policy in a firm not faced with scarce
resources. We shall assume that sufficient information is available to
the firm to enable it to estimate the demand functions for (and costs of)
its products. Subsequent calculations imply a precision that is rarely
justified in practice. Nevertheless, they are useful because they
illustrate the factors that are relevant to pricing decisions and the ways
in which the factors interact. In practice, in making the pricing model
explicit, assumptions and inter-relationships that have previously been
implicit will probably be exposed, leading to more enlightened and
maybe better decisions.

Jenned Ltd manufactures two products, Wye and Zed, in its
Beta Division. According to last year's divisional accounts the Beta
Division made a loss and for the coming year the company wishes to
establish a plan for the division that will avoid a recurrence of this
event. The company's calculation of the present selling prices of the
two products is given in Table 9.2. The direct costs in the statement are
calculated on an external opportunity cost basis. They are not expected
to alter during the coming year. There are no interdependences
between either the production or demand functions of the two
products.

Total overheads charged to the division last year amounted to
approximately 100% of the division's total direct costs. As a result an
allocation rate of 100% of total direct cost is being applied at present
to find the unit overhead cost of Wye and Zed. Further investigation
reveals that part of the total overhead cost charged to the division
relates to divisional fixed costs that will be avoided if the division's
production ceases. The remainder is an allocation of head office

Table 9.2

	Wye p	Zed p
Direct cost per unit:		
Labour	8.00	3.50
Materials	13.00	7.00
Machine user cost	15.00	4.00
Total direct cost per unit:	36.00	14.50
Overhead cost per unit:		
100% on total direct cost	36.00	14.50
Total cost per unit:	72.00	29.00
Profit mark-up:		
15% on total cost	10.80	4.35
Selling price per unit:		
(rounded to the nearest p)	83	33

administrative costs which will be unaffected by any decision regarding the Beta Division. In the coming year divisional fixed costs are expected to amount to £12,000 and Beta's allocation of head office administration expenses has been set provisionally at £10,500.

The profit mark-up represents a percentage return on cost that is regarded as being reasonable for the Beta division's two products.

The company has recently completed a market research study of the demand for its products. The figures relating to Wye and Zed are given in Table 9.3. They show the maximum likely sales volumes for the various prices given.[12] The demand curves implied by the survey are shown by the solid lines on the graphs in Figure 9.2. The problem is to formulate a plan for Beta Division for the coming year that will maximise the company's cash resources. The pricing policy for Wye and Zed will be a part of this plan.

12. In practice a more sophisticated treatment of the uncertainty surrounding these figures may be desirable. To illustrate the principles involved we shall assume that the sales volumes are the certain maxima that can be sold at the relevant selling prices.

Table 9.3

					Product Wye						*Product Zed*		
Price (p)	60	65	70	75	80	85	25	$27\frac{1}{2}$	30	$32\frac{1}{2}$	35	$37\frac{1}{2}$
Sales volume (000's)	37.5	35	30	25	20	15	85	80	75	70	65	60

As there are no interdependences between the two products and no scarce resources we may analyse the optimal output levels and prices for them individually. Subsequently we must consider the overall requirement that the sum of the contributions from both products must at least cover the divisional fixed costs if the Beta Division is to provide a contribution to head office fixed costs and profit.

The sales price–volume relationship for product Wye differs for output levels above and below 35,000; it exhibits a kink at that point. For our initial analysis we shall assume that it is constant for all output levels, further adjustment will be necessary only if the optimal output suggested by the calculation is more than 35,000 units. A linear extrapolation of the demand curve shows that it intersects the

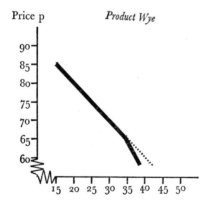

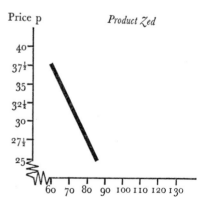

Volume demanded 000's

Volume demanded 000's

FIGURE 9.2

price axis at a price of 100p.[13] The slope of the curve reflects the reduction in selling price expected if one more unit is sold. The price function for Wye may be expressed

$$SPW = 100 - 0.001y$$

where SPW is the selling price and y the sales volume of product Wye. We can calculate the marginal revenue (MRW) of product Wye from the selling price equation:[14]

$$MRW = 100 - 0.002y.$$

The marginal cost of product Wye (MCW) in this case is the direct cost of 36p shown in Table 9.2. To find the optimal output level we must find the value of y that equates MRW and MCW:

$$100 - 0.002y = 36$$
$$y = 32,000.$$

The maximum price at which this output can be sold is found by substituting the optimal value of y in the selling price equation:

$$SPW = 100 - 0.001(32,000)$$
$$SPW = 68\text{p}.$$

A similar procedure will yield the optimal sales volume and selling price for product Zed. The price function for Zed is

$$SPZ = 67.5 - 0.0005z$$

---

13. For each price increase of 5p the volume demanded falls by 5,000 units. From the graph in Figure 9.2 it is apparent that at a volume of 15,000 the price is 85p. Therefore to reduce the volume to zero a price increase of 15,000/5,000 × 5p, that is 15p is required, giving a price of 100p.
14. TRW (Total revenue) $= SPW \cdot y = 100y - 0.001y^2$.

$$MRW = \frac{\mathrm{d}TRW}{\mathrm{d}y} = 100 - 0.002y.$$

Alternatively we could have used the general marginal revenue equation derived earlier in this chapter, [expression (1)].

where *SPZ* is the selling price and *z* the sales volume of Zed.[15] From this we can calculate the marginal revenue (*MRZ*) of product Zed:[16]

$$MRZ = 67.5 - 0.001z.$$

The marginal cost (*MCZ*) is $14\frac{1}{2}p$, as shown in Table 9.2, and the

Table 9.4

	Product Wye		Product Zed
Optimal output level	32,000		53,000
Selling price per unit	68p		41p
External opportunity cost per unit	36p		$14\frac{1}{2}$p
Unit contribution to divisional fixed costs	32p		$26\frac{1}{2}$p
Total contribution to divisional fixed costs:			
Wye 32,000 × 32p		£10,240	
Zed 53,000 × $26\frac{1}{2}$p		14,045	
		24,285	
Divisional fixed costs		12,000	
Divisional contribution to head office fixed costs and profit		12,285	

15. As each price increase of $2\frac{1}{2}$p results in a fall in the volume demanded of 5,000 units and as the volume is 60,000 at a price of $37\frac{1}{2}$p, the price increase needed to reduce the volume demanded from this level to zero is 60,000/5,000 × $2\frac{1}{2}$p, i.e., 30p, giving a price of $67\frac{1}{2}$p. The slope of the curve again reflects the reduction in selling price expected if one extra unit is sold.

16. *TRZ* (Total revenue) = $SPZ \cdot z = 67.5z - 0.0005z^2$.

$$MRZ = \frac{\mathrm{d}TRZ}{dz} = 67.5 - 0.001z.$$

Again, we could have used expression (1) to calculate *MRZ* directly.

Table 9.5

	Product Wye	Product Zed
Implied output level[17]	17,000	69,000
Selling price per unit	83p	33p
External opportunity cost per unit	36p	$14\frac{1}{2}$p
Unit contribution to divisional fixed costs	47p	$18\frac{1}{2}$p
Total contribution to divisional fixed costs:		
Wye 17,000 × 47p	£ 7,990	
Zed 69,000 × $18\frac{1}{2}$p	12,765	
	20,755	
Divisional fixed costs	12,000	
Divisional contribution to head office fixed costs and profits	8,755	

optimal output level is the value of z that equates MRZ and MCZ:

$$67.5 - 0.001z = 14.5$$
$$z = 53,000.$$

The optimal selling price for this output is found by substituting the optimal value of z in the selling price equation:

$$SPZ = 67.5 - 0.0005(53,000)$$
$$SPZ = 41p.$$

The optimal output level and selling price for product Zed are outside the range of the market research survey. We shall assume at

17. Found by solving for y and z respectivly in the selling price equations:
$$SPW = 100 - 0.001y$$
$$83 = 100 - 0.001y$$
$$y = 17,000$$
$$SPZ = 67.5 - 0.0005z$$
$$33 = 67.5 - 0.0005z$$
$$z = 69,000.$$

present that they are as valid as the observations within the range of the survey. We should point out to those responsible for adopting the plan that a further study may be necessary to confirm that the assumed demand relationship remains valid at the new level.

The production plan and contribution to head office fixed costs and profit implied by the above calculations are shown in Table 9.4. Jenned Ltd should set a price of 68p for Wye and 41p for Zed and plan to produce 32,000 units of the former and 53,000 units of the latter. The plan implied by the present selling prices of 83p and 33p is shown in Table 9.5. It is clear that this plan is sub-optimal in terms of the company's assumed objective for it yields a lower contribution to head office fixed costs and profit than does the new plan.

The above example illustrates how a company might tackle pricing problems where none of its resources is scarce. It outlines the sort of information that will be required. Pricing policy where one or more of a firm's resources is scarce is more complicated. Normally, a more refined programming approach than the one discussed in Chapter 7 is required. Such programming techniques, able to handle non-linear marginal revenue curves, are available but a study of them is outside the scope of this text.[18]

18. For an introduction to non-linear programming techniques see BAUMOL,
    W J, Economic Theory and Operations Analysis, 2nd Edition,
    Prentice-Hall, 1965, pages 210–30.

10 Some Specialised Analytical Models

In this chapter we shall consider briefly four further models or analytical methods that follow from the principles developed earlier and may be of particular interest to decision makers. The methods outlined are selected as representative of a large number of techniques that have emerged during the past few decades and embody the principles of decision making described in this book.

10.1 Decision Trees[1]

Decision trees provide a useful means of enumerating decision alternatives and linking them with environmental conditions and outcomes diagrammatically. The name stems from the form of the analysis which involves plotting possible courses of action as branches from some starting point. The general form of a decision tree, illustrated in Figure 10.1, may be applied to a variety of business problems. The boxes indicate points at which decisions have to be taken. The branches emanating from them indicate the available alternatives. The circles

1. A leading articles in this area is MAGEE, J F, 'Decision Trees for Decision Making', *Harvard Business Review*, July–August, 1964. For further examples see KEMENY, J G, SCHLEIFER, A, SNELL, J L and THOMPSON, G L, Finite Mathematics with Business Applications, Prentice-Hall, 1962, pages 25–8.

indicate points at which environmental changes, normally outside the control of the decision maker, may affect the consequences of prior decisions. The branches from these points enumerate the various main types of environment (state of the world) that may ensue. Where

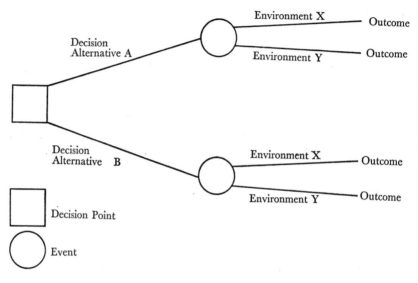

FIGURE 10.1

there is more than one possible environment it may be helpful to assign probabilities (i.e. likelihood of occurrence) to each one at each stage, to facilitate the task of the decision maker. Decisions and events may occur in any sequence, and there is no limit, other than a computational one, to the number of decisions and events that may be included in the tree before the ultimate range of outcomes is determined.

A decision tree analysis is not in itself a solution technique but rather a means of clarifying for the decision maker the range of alternatives available and their possible consequences. As such, it is normally used in conjunction with an acceptable method of project appraisal, perhaps along the lines of the various decision rules developed earlier in this text.

Where the problem is complex, giving rise to a large number of branches, it may be necessary to 'prune' the tree if it is not to become unwieldy. This may be achieved, for example, by eliminating routes that are clearly inferior to others representing alternative courses of action. The quality of decision making and the decision maker's insight into the problems confronting him may be improved merely by the discipline imposed in constructing the tree and, if necessary, in pruning it.

Table 10.1

Year	Product A £000's	Product B £000's
1	6.5	4.0
2	8.0	5.0
3	6.0	3.0
4	3.5	6.5
5	4.5	4.0

Let us consider an example in which, for the sake of simplicity, the possibility of uncertain environments is ignored.[2] In other words, the decision tree will link only decision points. Suppose that a company, Sagittarius Ltd, manufactures two products, *A* and *B*. Factory capacity and production conditions are such that it is only worthwhile making one of the products in any one year. Because of manufacturing difficulties *A* cannot be produced for two or more years consecutively. No such restriction applies to *B*.[3] The company expects the demand for both products to cease after five years but wishes to know which to produce in each of the five years until then. Table 10.1 shows the total contribution Sagittarius Ltd expects from each product if it is made in any of the next five years. We shall assume that the time value of money has been allowed for in the figures in Table 10.1, i.e. that the figures are expressed in present value terms.

2. The treatment of the problem of uncertainty is not amongst the main concerns of this text. For some introductory remarks see Chapter 1, pages 6–9.

3. A practical example of this sort of situation might be found in agriculture, where particular crops may not be grown for two years consecutively on the same plot of land.

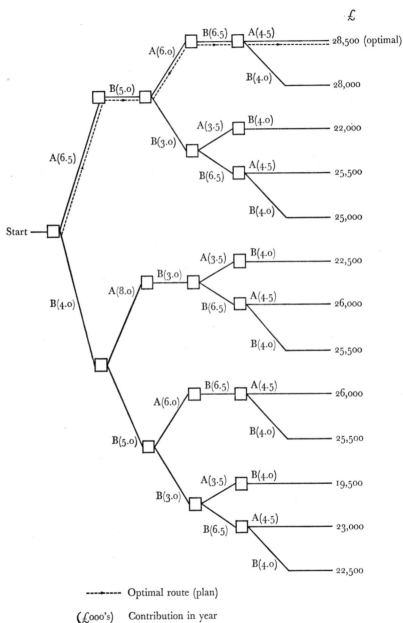

Year   1   2   3   4   5   *Total Contribution*

£

B(6.5)   A(4.5)   28,500 (optimal)

A(6.0)

B(4.0)   28,000

B(5.0)

B(3.0)

A(3.5)   B(4.0)   22,000

B(6.5)   A(4.5)   25,500

B(4.0)   25,000

A(6.5)

Start

B(4.0)

A(8.0)

B(3.0)

A(3.5)   B(4.0)   22,500

B(6.5)   A(4.5)   26,000

B(4.0)   25,500

B(5.0)

A(6.0)

B(6.5)   A(4.5)   26,000

B(4.0)   25,500

B(3.0)

A(3.5)   B(4.0)   19,500

B(6.5)   A(4.5)   23,000

B(4.0)   22,500

------- Optimal route (plan)

(£000's)   Contribution in year

FIGURE 10.2   156

The problem is shown as a decision tree in Figure 10.2. There are thirteen possible sets of decisions, leading to total contributions over the five year period ranging from £19,500 to £28,500. From the decision tree we see that the maximum contribution of £28,500 results from production of A in year 1, B in year 2, A in year 3, B in year 4 and A in year 5. No other plan yields as high a contribution. The decision tree also provides information about the range of possible outcomes and illustrates the effect of the constraint imposed because the company is unable to produce A in two consecutive years. The tree identifies the pattern; the choice of a production plan is made by using familiar costing principles, embodied in the measurement of contributions.

10.2   Dynamic Programming[4]

In its simplest form, dynamic programming is an extension of the decision tree analysis considered in the previous section. It may be appropriate where a number of sequential decisions have to be taken concerning an activity that may be divided into stages. It is particularly useful where a decision tree would involve so many possible routes as to become practically unmanageable. Let us reconsider the case of Sagittarius Ltd discussed in the previous section. The objective is to find that route which yields the highest total contribution over a five year period.

The routes available are described in Figure 10.3 in a way that differs from the presentation in Figure 10.2. Each stage, indicated by a number in a box, implies a possible decision point. The lines emanating from each decision point trace the alternative courses of action available. At stage 7 (the box containing the number 7), for example, having produced B in year 3, Sagittarius Ltd must decide what to produce in year 4. There are two alternatives, A and B. The contribution figures on the lines represent the contributions that are expected if the course of action implied by a particular line is followed. For example, if the company is at stage 7, having produced B in year

---

4. See for example, WHITE, D J, Dynamic Programming, Oliver and Boyd, 1968; and WHITE, D J, DONALDSON, W A and LAWRIE, N L, Operational Research Techniques, Business Books, 1969, Chapter 3.

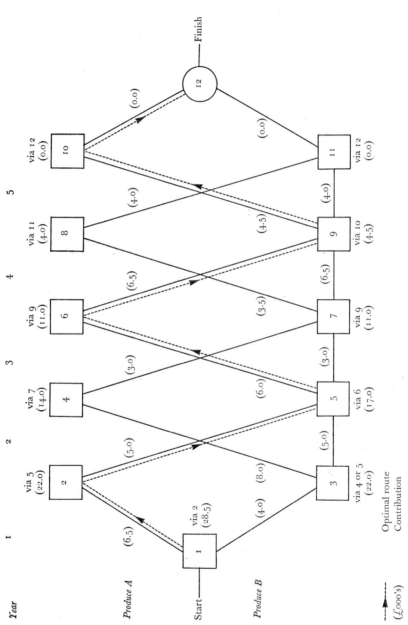

FIGURE 10.3

3, it can either move to stage 8 in year 4, producing A with an expected contribution for the year of £3,500, or to stage 9, producing B again, now with an anticipated contribution of £6,500. The total number of routes from start to finish implied by Figure 10.3 is thirteen, as was the case with the decision tree analysis of the same problem.

The optimal production plan was derived from the decision tree by calculating the total contribution from each route and choosing the highest. This technique becomes excessively lengthy when many routes are involved. Dynamic programming provides a more concise method of solution. The principle applied in solution is to work backwards, in our example from year 5, calculating the optimal path available from each stage successively, ignoring any decisions that might be made for prior years. This approach is consistent with the argument developed in previous chapters that past decisions are normally not relevant in choosing between future courses of action, except to the extent that they determine the starting position.

Let us consider Figure 10.3 further. At the end of year 5 (stages 10 and 11) no further production of A or B is worthwhile as the demand for both products is expected to cease. Thus anticipated future production and contribution are both zero, which is the position represented by stage 12. From either stage 10 or 11 the best, and only, path forward is to stage 12. Now let us move backwards to consider stages 8 and 9, representing the available decision points at the end of year 4. From stage 8 only one course of action is available for year 5, the production of B, as A cannot be manufactured for two consecutive years. The only route forward is via stage 11. The maximum cumulative contribution possible from stage 8 to the finish is found by summing the cumulative contribution at stage 11 (£0) and the contribution expected in moving from stage 8 to stage 11 (£4,000). This cumulative contribution is noted by stage 8 on the diagram.

From stage 9 two activities are available, produce A (move to stage 10) and produce B (move to stage 11). The former yields a cumulative contribution of £4,500 (£4,500 + £0) and the latter £4,000 (£4,000 + £0). The best route from stage 9 is via stage 10 and this is noted on the diagram by stage 9, together with the associated cumulative contribution. The procedure is continued, working backwards through the diagram until stage 1, the initial decision point, is reached.

From here the company may move to either stage 2 or stage 3. The former produces an expected total contribution of £28,500 (£6,500 + £22,000) and the latter £26,000 (£4,000 + £22,000). The optimal first move is to stage 2, implying production of A in year 1. From stage 2 the optimal route is to stage 5 and thence to stages 6, 9, 10 and 12 as marked by the broken line in Figure 10.3. The production plan implied is identical with that determined from the decision tree. The solution process, however, is likely to be quicker for complex problems.

10.3 *Critical Path Analysis*[5]

Critical path analysis is an aid to the scheduling of complex projects where they can be analysed into a number of activities, some of which are performed sequentially and others in parallel. It enables the decision maker to identify critical activities that are most likely to delay completion of a project. The project itself may be described in the form of a network. The following symbols are conventionally used in network analysis:

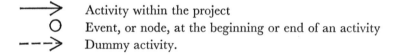

Activity within the project
Event, or node, at the beginning or end of an activity
Dummy activity.

Each activity has a time associated with it. The network is constructed so that sequential and parallel activities are shown clearly. It may be that one activity cannot be started until another is completed although the activities may not be directly linked by an activity line. In this situation normal practice is to insert a dummy activity, which has a zero time. Entry and exit points are conventionally shown on the network as lead and end activities although they are normally of zero duration.

5. See for example, WILSON, C, Operational Research for Students of Management, Intertext Books, 1970, Chapter 6; KEMENY, J G, SCHLEIFER, A, SNELL, J L and THOMPSON, G L, Finite Mathematics with Business Applications, Prentice-Hall, 1962, pages 72–9; and WHITE, D J, DONALDSON, W A and LAWRIE, N L, Operational Research Techniques, Business Books, 1969, Chapter 4.

We shall leave the world of business briefly for an example of critical path analysis.[6] Suppose that a family wishes to make a pot of tea and some ham sandwiches and would like to know what scheduling of the necessary activities will minimise the total time between start and finish. The activities to be performed and the time required for each are listed in Table 10.2. Certain sequential relationships are

Table 10.2

Activity	Time required (*minutes*)
A Boil kettle of water	2
B Slice bread	1
C Butter bread	$1\frac{1}{2}$
D Put ham on bread	$\frac{1}{2}$
E Heat teapot	$\frac{1}{2}$
F Put tea and boiling water in pot and allow to brew	2
G Put milk and sugar in cups	1
H Cut sandwiches	1
I Pour and stir tea	$\frac{1}{2}$

obvious from the table. For example, activity E cannot be performed until activity A is finished. One further condition imposed is that the tea should not be poured until the sandwiches are ready. This reduces the probability of the tea becoming cold. The whole operation is shown as a network in Figure 10.4. The required times are shown next to the activity letters. The nodes are traditionally numbered in such a way that activity lines always lead from lower to higher numbered nodes.

To compute the critical path through the network we first calculate earliest event times (EET's) for each node; that is, the earliest time it is possible to arrive at a particular node given the scheduling constraints that must be observed. Starting with the first node, which is presumed to have an EET of zero, we work from left to right. To calculate the EET of a node we add the time of each activity line

6. In fact, there are many cases in business where critical path analysis is applicable, in particular for analysing manufacturing schedules and audit programmes.

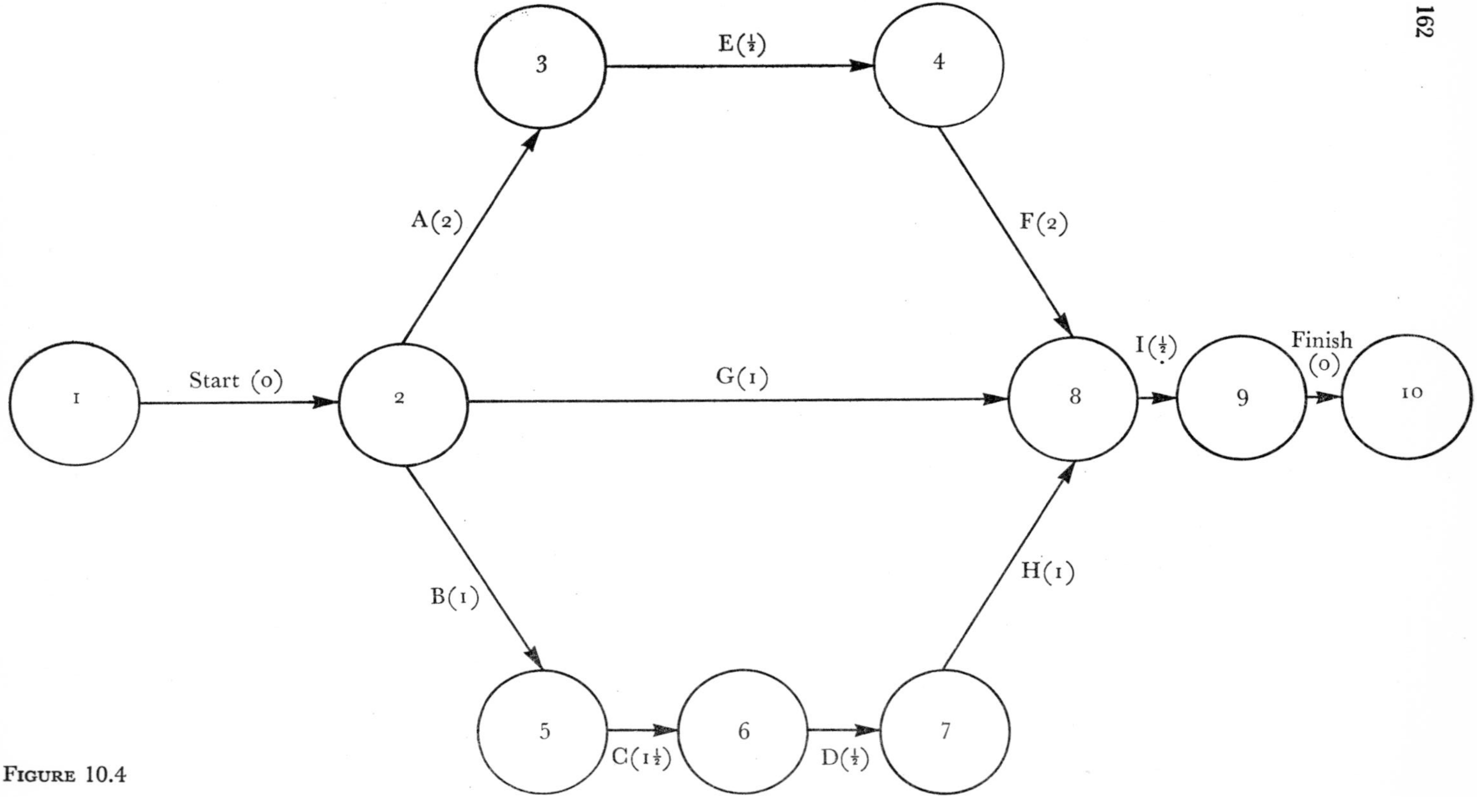

162

FIGURE 10.4

entering it to the EET of the node at the beginning of the activity; the highest resulting time is the EET of the node. In our example all but one of the nodes has only one activity line entering it. The exception is node 8 which has three. The EET of node 8 is the highest of $4\frac{1}{2}$, 1 and 4, that is $4\frac{1}{2}$.[7] The EET of each node is shown in Figure 10.5. Node 10 represents the finish of the operation and its EET of 5 minutes suggests that this is the shortest time in which the tea and sandwiches can be made.

This information is interesting but perhaps of more importance is a knowledge of those activities that are critical to the attainment of the shortest possible total activity time. In other words, it would be helpful to know those activities that, if delayed, are most likely to affect the completion time of the project. To determine this we shall calculate latest event times (LET's) for each node; that is, the latest time an activity leaving the node may begin (or an activity entering it may be completed) without delaying the earliest possible completion of the project.

To calculate the LET's we start with the node that represents the finish of the operation (node 10) and set its LET equal to its EET, i.e. 5 minutes. Then, working backwards through the network, we calculate the LET of each node by considering all activity lines leaving it and the LET's of the nodes at the end of the activities. The LET of the node is calculated by subtracting the time for each activity from the LET of the node at its end; the shortest time resulting is the LET of the node from which the activity lines emanate. Again only one node, number 2, has more than one activity line leaving it. The LET of this node is the lowest of 0 $(2 - 2)$, $3\frac{1}{2}$ $(4\frac{1}{2} - 1)$ and $\frac{1}{2}$ $(1\frac{1}{2} - 1)$, i.e. 0. The LET of each node is shown in Figure 10.5.

The critical activities (those where no scope is available for late starting or other delay) are those linking nodes whose EET's are equal

---

7. From Figure 10.5 it can be seen that three activity lines enter node 8. The line from node 4 represents an activity taking 2 minutes and the EET of node 4 is $2\frac{1}{2}$ minutes giving a total of $4\frac{1}{2}$ minutes. The activity line from node 2 represents a one minute activity which when added to the zero EET of node 2 gives 1 minute. The line from node 7 represents an activity of one minute which is added to the EET of node 7 (3 minutes) giving a total of 4 minutes.

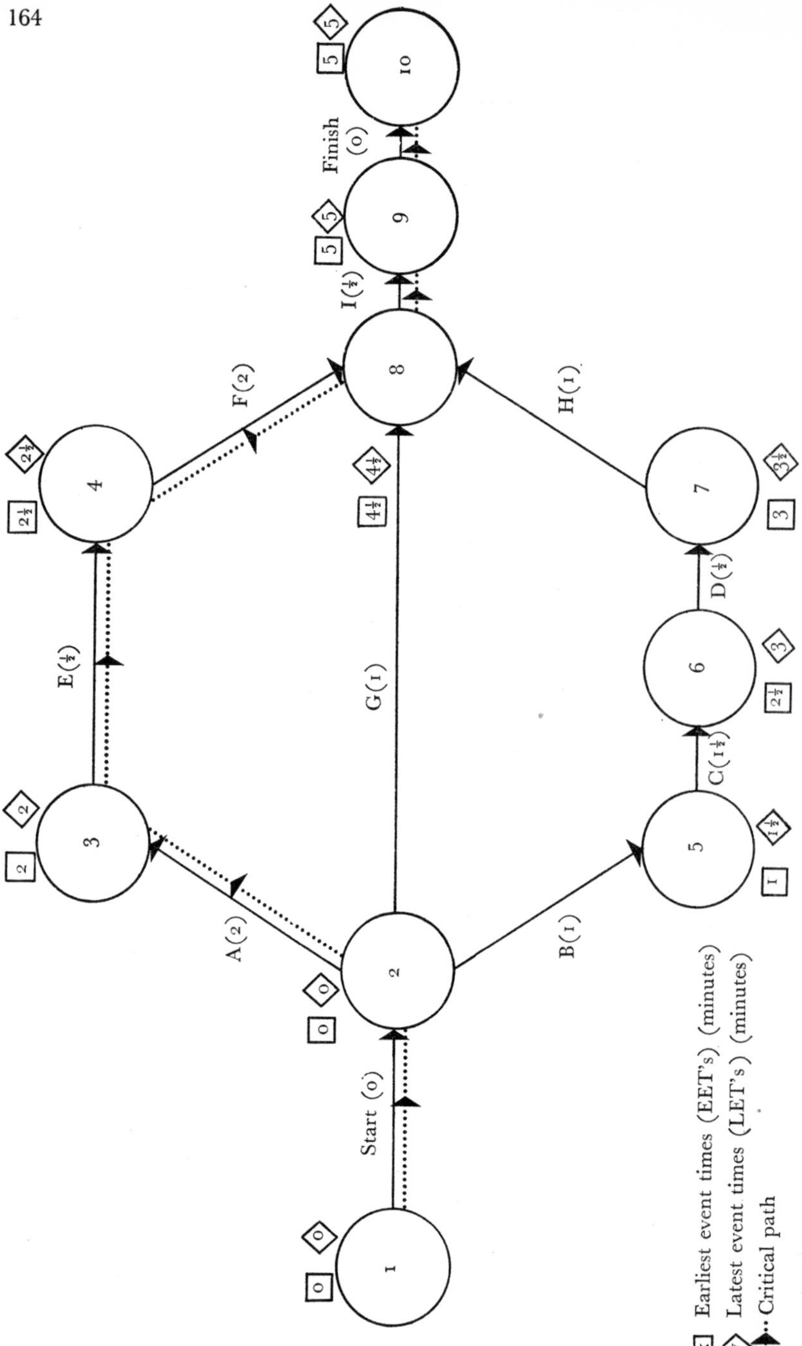

Earliest event times (EET's) (minutes)

Latest event times (LET's) (minutes)

···· Critical path

FIGURE 10.5

to their LET's. The critical path is defined as that comprising the critical activities. It is possible that there will be more than one critical path through the network. Any delay in a critical activity will result in a corresponding delay in completion of the project. The critical activities in our example are A (boiling water), E (heating teapot), F (brewing tea) and I (pouring and stirring tea) and the family's main consideration should be to ensure no unnecessary delays in these activities.

This is not to say that the other activities are unimportant. The degree of slack available on them may be small and a significant delay may affect the completion time of the project. Various types of 'float' may be used to measure the available slack on non-critical activities. For example we might define the float of an activity as the LET of the event succeeding the activity less the sum of the EET of the event preceding the activity and the duration of the activity itself. So the float for activity C would be $3 - (1 + 1\frac{1}{2})$ which equals $\frac{1}{2}$. Provided that no other activities are delayed so as to affect activity C, it could be commenced up to $\frac{1}{2}$ minute late or take up to $\frac{1}{2}$ minute longer than planned without delaying completion of the whole operation.

Although the example used here is a simple one it illustrates the value of critical path analysis in scheduling complex operations and in highlighting those activities whose durations critically affect the completion of a project. Use of the method may be extended. For example, if it is desired to reduce total time and if activity times may be reduced at known costs, critical path analysis can be used to calculate where reductions should be sought. A detailed consideration of this extended use is outside the scope of this text.

10.4 Inventory Control[8]

Inventory control, and, in particular, the optimal order or production

8. The following references represent a small proportion of those that could have been cited: PESTON, M H, 'The Elementary Ideas of Inventory Analysis', in BAXTER, W T and DAVIDSON, S (eds), Studies in Accounting Theory, Sweet and Maxwell, 1962; BAUMOL, W J, Economic Theory and Operations Analysis, 2nd Edition, Prentice-Hall, 1965, pages 5–10; and FARRAR, D E and MEYER, J R, Managerial Economics, Prentice-Hall, 1970, pages 17–22.

batch size problem, provides a useful illustration of the application of analytical methods to business problems, dealing in particular with the usefulness of incremental, or marginal, analysis in deriving optimal solutions to business problems.

Consider the case of J Doe, a retailer selling a wide range of products one of which is the Ozo. In the coming year Doe expects to sell 3,000 units of Ozo and wishes to minimise the total cost of acquiring and storing the necessary supplies. Sales of Ozo normally follow an even pattern throughout the year but to protect himself against possible deviations Doe keeps a minimum stock of 100 units.[9] Further supplies of Ozo are ordered whenever the stock falls to this minimum level and the time lag between ordering and delivery is small enough to be ignored. There are basically two types of cost associated with Ozo: ordering costs and holding costs. The former comprise two elements; a fixed cost of £50 per order to cover postage, clerical time, and the like (i.e. the amount does not vary with the size of the order), and a variable cost of 50p per unit which varies in direct proportion with the size of the order. Holding costs, for example storage costs, interest on capital required and warehouse handling costs, amount to £20 per annum for each unit of Ozo stored. They are related directly to the number of units of Ozo held.

In determining the stock re-order quantity that minimises total cost both the minimum stock level of 100 units and the direct cost of 50p per unit may be ignored. They will contribute the same amount to total cost whatever batch size is chosen and are not relevant to a decision on optimal re-order quantity although they may be important for other decisions. The conflict between the motivations caused by the other costs is shown in Figure 10.6. Total ordering costs may be reduced by increasing the batch size so that the £50 fixed cost is incurred fewer times during the year. On the other hand the larger the batch size the larger will be the average stock of Ozo and the higher will be the total holding cost for the year.

9. In a more refined model the minimum stock level could itself be the subject of analysis.

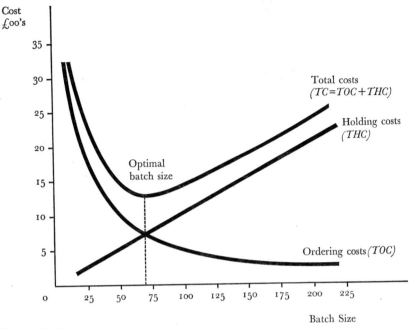

Cost £oo's (y-axis)

Total costs
(TC=TOC+THC)

Holding costs
(THC)

Optimal
batch size

Ordering costs (TOC)

Batch Size

FIGURE 10.6

At this stage, let us introduce some simple mathematical notation:

X Re-order quantity (batch size)
S Expected total units of sales in the year
f Fixed ordering costs per batch
h Annual holding costs per unit.

We may derive equations for total ordering costs (TOC) and total holding costs (THC) for the year. If each batch order comprises X units and a total of S units are required during the coming year then S/X batches will be required. The ordering costs amount to f per batch and the total ordering costs for the year may be written

$$TOC = f \cdot \frac{S}{X}$$

or substituting the figures for the example of Mr Doe

$$TOC = \pounds 50 \cdot \frac{1,000}{X} = \frac{\pounds 50,000}{X}.$$

As sales of Ozo are expected to follow an even pattern through the year stock will be 'used up' at a uniform rate and the average stock in store during the year, excluding the minimum buffer stock of 100 units, will be $X/2$. As each unit in store causes annual holding costs of h the total holding costs may be written

$$THC = h \cdot \frac{X}{2}$$

or in the case of Mr Doe

$$THC = £20 \cdot \frac{X}{2} = £10X.$$

The assumed objective is to minimise the total of stock ordering and holding costs. The total cost (TC) equation may be written

$$TC = TOC + THC$$

$$TC = f \cdot \frac{S}{X} + h \cdot \frac{X}{2}$$

or, in our example, as

$$TC = £\left(\frac{50,000}{X} + 10X\right).$$

The equations for TOC, THC and TC have been used to construct the cost functions in Figure 10.6. The optimal batch size is the value of X that minimises the TC function. For product Ozo, this value may be read from the graph in Figure 10.6, or, in the general case, we may calculate it by using the differential calculus. The batch size that minimises total cost is given by the formula:[10]

$$X = \sqrt{\frac{2fS}{h}}.$$

10. The formula is determined by differentiating TC with respect to X and setting the answer equal to zero:

$$\frac{\mathrm{d}TC}{\mathrm{d}X} = \frac{-fS}{X^2} + \frac{h}{2} = 0$$

$$X = \sqrt{\frac{2fS}{h}}$$

The general solution may be applied to any stock ordering problem with similar characteristics to that of J Doe. The optimal re-order quantity for Ozo may be found by substitution in the general solution

$$X = \sqrt{\frac{2(50 \times 1,000)}{20}}$$

$$X = \pm 71$$

to the nearest whole number. The optimal batch size is 71.[11]

As in previous examples the suitability of the model depends on the validity of the assumptions made. The direct cost of Ozo units

---

To confirm that we are at a minimum (rather than a maximum) we must check that the second order condition is satisfied, i.e., that it is positive:

$$\frac{d^2 TC}{dX^2} = \frac{2fS}{X^3}$$

As f and S are constant and positive the second order condition is satisfied provided that X is positive.

11. As an alternative, we might have used trial and error to determine the optimal batch size. Using the formulas for total ordering costs (TOC) and total holding costs (THC) we get:

Batch Size	TOC $\left(\dfrac{£50,000}{X}\right)$ £	THC $+ £10X$ £	Total Cost $= \left(\dfrac{£50,000}{X} + £10X\right)$ £
.	.	.	.
.	.	.	.
40	1,250	400	1,650
50	1,000	500	1,500
60	833	600	1,433
70	714	700	1,414
80	625	800	1,425
90	556	900	1,456
100	500	1,000	1,500
.	.	.	.
.	.	.	.

The table suggests that the optimal batch size is between 60 and 80 units. Further trial and error analysis will produce the figure of 71 units. The table also shows that between batch sizes of 50 and 100 units there is little change in total cost, information not provided by the optimal batch size formula.

may vary according to the batch size; for example, large batches may lead to quantity discounts. Holding costs may not be a direct linear function of the average stock level, there may be economies of scale, scarce warehouse capacity and other factors affecting the opportunity cost. In addition the model is based on assumptions of steady demand and no delivery delays, both of which may be inappropriate. The model might be adapted to meet these difficulties. Even in its simplest form it should provide those responsible for inventory control with some insight into the nature of the costs they must consider.

11 Conclusion

11.1 A Brief Review

The central theme of this text has been to argue the merits of
opportunity cost as a measure of the economic costs and consequences
of investment decisions. This emphasis is significant. Traditional
accounting conventions are persistently used to provide measures of
costs and benefits in decision making situations. These conventions
were developed for other purposes (tax assessment, dividend law,
certain stewardship functions and so on) and are not necessarily
relevant for decision making. An incremental approach is required
to reflect the change in a firm's position resulting from pursuing a
particular course of action.

In this text we have considered the application of the
opportunity cost concept to a number of decisions including
accept/reject decisions, pricing policy, output level decisions and cost
estimation, together with the optimal use of scarce resources. We have
been concerned primarily with short-term decision methodology. The
problem of allocating resources *over time* is the subject of another text
in this series.[1] The models that have been discussed are not presented

1. CARSBERG, B V, Analysis for Investment Decisions, Haymarket Publishing,
   forthcoming.

as panaceas but rather as general guidelines to provide those responsible for making decisions with a greater degree of insight and understanding into the problems facing them. We hope that this will lead to an improvement in the quality of the decisions they make. In this final chapter other major areas, worthy of study by anyone interested in decision making, are introduced and certain general assumptions that have been implicit throughout the text are reconsidered briefly.

11.2 Control

We have discussed at some length the derivation of optimal business plans but have not considered the problems inherent in the implementation and control of these plans. Simply stated, control comprises the frequent comparison of actual results with planned performance and the subsequent investigation of variances. As control implies comparison it is important that like should be compared with like if the analysis is to be meaningful. Thus the control devices utilised should be in a form consistent with the models used for planning.[2]

There are primarily two purposes of control systems. The first is to motivate those responsible for implementing the organisational plans. Control for its own sake is valueless and meaningless, the information that administrative overheads exceeded budget by £10,000 is of little use unless it in some way influences the future performance of the firm. This leads us to the second purpose of control systems: to provide an organisation with information that will enable it to improve the quality of its performance in the future. A good control system will include a frequent consideration and, if necessary, revision of organisational plans. In this context it is clear that planning and control is essentially an iterative process and to decide upon an optimal plan is merely the first step in a procedure that will continue as long as the firm exists.

In devising a control system the questions must also be asked: control of whom? control of what? There are numerous areas within

2. For an application of the principle of opportunity cost to standard costing systems see BROMWICH, M, 'Standard Costing for Planning and Control', *The Accountant*, April 19, April 26 and May 3, 1969.

the total financial system where control is necessary. Some of these are considered in detail in another text in this series.[3]

11.3 Behavioural Effects of Budgets[4]

In the previous section we mentioned briefly the need to motivate those responsible for implementing company budgets. The behavioural effects of planning and control have been largely neglected by accounting writers until recently and yet the problem of persuading employees to accept budgets and to incorporate organisational goals into their personal aspiration levels is crucial to the success of the firm. Much of the debate in the behavioural literature is concerned with the degree to which employees should be allowed to participate in setting plans and with the extent to which budgets should be strictly imposed on them by systems of rewards and punishments.

The basic argument on one side runs that by imposing budgets on employees, without giving them the opportunity to participate in their setting or comment on their applicability, the firm is running the risk of creating pressures and internal conflict amongst its employees which may lead to a reduction in their efficiency. It may also be creating a situation where each department strives to achieve its budget target without regard for possible repercussions on other departments (for example if there are interdependences between two or more departments), or where individuals eventually begin to blame the budget for all manner of unrelated problems and, consequently, make little attempt to solve them.

The effect of pressure seems to be the most significant of the likely consequences. Counter-forces may appear to combat the pressure, including agreements between employees not to work hard, resentment against (and refusal to comply with) the budget and those responsible for setting it, and so on. As the pressure is increased, so these counter-forces increase to maintain an equilibrium. Some writers have suggested that performance may be more efficiently improved by

3. TOMKINS, C, Evaluation of Divisional Performance, Haymarket Publishing, forthcoming.
4. For a fuller treatment of this area see HOPWOOD, A G, Accounting and Human Behaviour, Haymarket Publishing, forthcoming.

reducing the counter-pressures than by increasing the pressures.[5] One way of achieving this might be by granting employees participation rights at the budget-setting stage. If successful this should lead to an increase in morale. This in turn should lead to the acceptance of budget goals into individual aspiration levels which will result in increased productivity.

This line of reasoning has been disputed.[6] The counter-argument agrees that participation may lead to an increase in morale but disputes that this necessarily implies increased productivity. A happy labour force may not be an efficient one. Stedry suggests that two sets of budgets are required; a 'realistic' set to be used for forecasting and planning and a second set to be revealed to employees and used to motivate them. The second set of budgets should be aimed at a higher level of performance than the first so that employees striving for the higher performance are more likely to reach the expected level. The dangers of this approach include the consequences of the discovery by employees that such a system is in operation (e.g. a lack of credibility and a policy of non-co-operation in the future) and the adverse effects on morale of continually failing to achieve budget performance (the intended consequence of the system).

A choice between these theories requires a study of the empirical evidence available. Unfortunately proponents of both theories have produced evidence that seems to support their own views. The problem of empirical testing in the behavioural area is that individuals tend to react not only to the changes occasioned by the experiment but also to the fact that they are themselves the subjects of the observations. The conflicting nature of the evidence suggests that different approaches may be optimal in different firms, depending upon the size and framework of the organisation, the nature

5. See, for example, ARGYRIS, C, 'Human Problems with Budgets', *Harvard Business Review*, Vol. 31, No. 1, January–February, 1953; and BECKER, S and GREEN, D, 'Budgeting and Employee Behavior', *Journal of Business*, Vol. 35, No. 4, October, 1962.
6. See, for example, STEDRY, A C, 'Budgetary Control: A Behavioral Approach', in ALEXIS, M and WILSON, C Z, Organizational Decision Making, Prentice-Hall, 1967.

of its employees and so on. Behaviourism is still in its infancy; significant developments may well prove of great value to business.

11.4 *Simulation*[7]

Many of the models that have been discussed in this text are what may be called algorithmic models. They involve the derivation of an algorithm that, in its general form, may be applied to a variety of firms and problems with similar characteristics. Once the algorithm is derived a particular numerical solution is obtained by substituting the relevant data for the particular problem into the general formula. An alternative, or, perhaps more commonly, a complementary approach is provided by simulation. The simulation approach involves building a specific model for each problem or organisation in contrast to the general solutions of algorithmic methods. The distinction between the two approaches is, in practice, rarely clear cut. Similar principles and methodology are relevant to both and the best results are frequently obtained by a combination of the two.

Because of its specific nature a simulation approach is often better able to accommodate quirks and peculiarities of particular problems. In a generalised method of solution these normally have to be treated as exceptions to the general rule. The flexibility of a simulation approach may be illustrated by considering the optimal stock re-order quantity problem discussed in Chapter 10. An implicit assumption of our model was that re-ordering is effected whenever the stock of Ozo falls to its minimum level, i.e. the re-order time is treated as a continuous variable. In practice, stock re-order may only be possible at discrete time intervals, say at the beginning of a week. A simulation approach has no difficulty in handling discrete variables

7. For an introduction to simulation methods see NAYLOR, T H, and others, Computer Simulation Techniques, John Wiley & Sons, 1966, Chapters 1 and 2; ROBERTS, E B, 'Industrial Dynamics and the Design of Management Control Systems', in BONINI, C P, JAEDICKE, R K and WAGNER, H M (eds), Management Controls: New Directions in Basic Research, McGraw-Hill, 1964; and FORRESTER, J W, Industrial Dynamics, Boston Massachusetts Institute of Technology, 1961, particularly Preface and Chapters 1 and 4.

like this and in consequence may be less hampered by the need for simplifying assumptions to reduce the problem to workable proportions.

On the other hand, the 'set-up cost' of a simulation model is incurred on each occasion a firm is faced with a particular type of problem, for which it has not previously developed a simulation model.

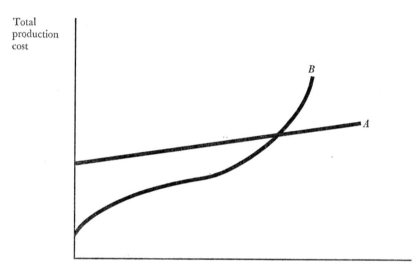

FIGURE 11.1

The model is particularised for the problem. An algorithmic model, because of its more generalised nature, may usually be applied to a wider range of problems, thus often reducing the cost of setting up a model for a particular problem. However, if the problem involves complex relationships that cannot reasonably be approximated by more simple ones, simulation may provide a more satisfactory method of solution.

Consider the two cost–volume relationships shown in Figure 11.1. If costs appear to behave in the manner described by A a formula may be derived simply to fit the (linear) curve. But the equation required for B will be more complex and may make an algorithmic solution difficult. Simulation handles both functions in essentially the same manner; total production cost data at various output levels are used to produce a range of possible outcomes to guide the decision maker. Unlike the algorithmic case an unique optimal numerical solution is not guaranteed. This itself may be an advantage for it avoids the sometimes illusory precision of an algorithmic solution, which is unlikely to provide a greater degree of accuracy than is attached to the input data used.

Although still a relatively little developed method, simulation is becoming accepted as a complement to other analytical methods and, in some cases, as a substitute for them.

11.5 General Limitations Reviewed

Certain general conditions, which may often be inapplicable in practice, have been assumed throughout this text. We shall reconsider these briefly for it is important that the models developed should be seen in their proper context, including any limitations that have been imposed by the assumptions.

The first general restriction is that the problems peculiar to resource allocation over time have not been considered. The text is primarily concerned with short-term decision methodology. In Chapter 2 (pages 22–23) a decision rule, called the net present value rule, was developed for the acceptance or rejection of particular opportunities. One important factor in applying this rule is an indication of the rate at which a firm or individual would be willing to exchange resources in one period for resources in another, that is the interest or discount rate to be applied.

In Chapter 1 (pages 6–9) the problem of risk and uncertainty was introduced. For example, a course of action which shows a high return based on single figure 'best guesses', but which has a wide range of possible outcomes, may, in practice, be passed over for an alternative with a lower 'expected' return and a smaller range of possible outcomes. All decisions are concerned with choices between future courses of action and the future is never certain. Thus all decisions are based on data that, to some degree, are uncertain. The approaches suggested in this text to various short-term decision problems are not invalidated by the existence of uncertainty, but the results must be interpreted with caution for they are unlikely to be better then the quality of the (uncertain) input data used.

Finally, it should be remembered that we have been primarily concerned with decision making in the private sector. The assumed objectives and consequent decision rules are those that seem likely to apply to private firms and individuals. The methodological approach to public sector decisions is not essentially different. An objective or set of objectives exist that govern the establishment of criteria for project appraisal. However, if public sector objectives differ from those assumed to relate to private firms, the decision rules to be used will also differ. There are non-financial costs and benefits that private firms more often ignore than public sector organisations, and therefore different evaluation rules might be needed in the two sectors. The basic principles are similar but their application may differ.

The models developed in this book are not ideal for practical application. Nor are any others that are available as aids to decision makers at the present time. However, the difficulties encountered in the past are being gradually overcome; for example, experience in handling factors that are not easily quantified has led to decision makers including more of these factors as quantifiables in a decision analysis. Those who develop decision (and other) models learn most about the weaknesses and usefulness of the models by observing their application in practice. Those who recommend and those who implement should be great allies!

Index